Borrego Beginnings

Early Days in the Borrego Valley

1910-1960

(2) Agriculture
- Alfalpha (11 cuttings)
- Dates
- Tomatoes
- cucumbers
- melons

Failures
- Pecans
- cabbage

"beating the markets"

- Albert Ahern
- AA BURNANDS

1940's

(1.)
Big picture

- Borrego (1930's)
(1) - Borrego Springs (1950's) } 2 diff places
(resort)

(2) Agriculture Key to the economy

(3) 1st cattlemen
- then homesteaders

Borrego Beginnings

Early Days in the Borrego Valley 1910-1960

Fred Lang "tomato" King

by Phil Brigandi

Doc Beatty
- school board
- voting precinct
- Chamber of Commerce Board
- Truckhaven Rd. & Yaqui Pass Rd.

Published by
Anza-Borrego Desert Natural History Association
Borrego Springs, California

Edited by: Ollie Cone & Betsy Knaak
Designed by: Linda Weisler of VisComm
Project Coordination by: Betsy Knaak

Printed in the United States of America

Library of Congress Cataloging-in-Publication Data

Brigandi, Phil, 1959-
Borrego beginnings: early days in the Borrego Valley, 1910-1960 / by Phil Brigandi.—1st ed.
p. cm.—(Borrego Desert heritage series; v. 2)
Includes bibliographical references and index.
ISBN 0-910805-10-5
1. Borrego Springs Region (Calif.)—History—20th century. 2. Borrego Springs Region (Calif.)—Social life and customs—20th century. I. Title. II. Series.

F869.B68 B75 2001
979.4'98—dc21

2001035740

Anza-Borrego Desert Natural History Association is a 501(c)3 nonprofit organization dedicated to educational, scientific and historical endeavors pertaining to the Borrego Desert and surrounding region. Our publications are an educational service intended to enhance the public's understanding and enjoyment of the desert. If you would like to know more about our publications, memberships, our Borrego Desert Nature Center, lectures, guided hikes and other projects, please contact: Anza-Borrego Desert Natural History Association, P.O. Box 310, Borrego Springs, CA 92004; (760) 767-3052; or www.abdnha.org.

Cover photo: *Eddie DuVall's Borego Valley store and post office, 1938.*

TABLE OF CONTENTS

DEDICATION

PHIL BRIGANDI

For Lelah Porter
Borego Pioneer

FOREWORD

Picture an isolated little desert community, connected to the outside world by just a few winding dirt roads. Agriculture is key to the local economy, but a few tourists are starting to come, many attracted by the annual wildflower bloom. There's a school and a post office, a chamber of commerce and an American Legion Post. It's a tight-knit community where residents must invent their own entertainment. Is it the little homesteader community of Borego in the 1930s, or the new resort town of Borrego Springs in the 1950s?

It could be either. Borego and Borrego Springs are linked not only by place, but in the way both communities developed. This is not to say that Borrego Springs has not grown far beyond anything Borego's early settlers ever could have imagined, but without Borego's pioneer homesteaders, there most likely never would have been a Borrego Springs.

Until the 1940s, the Borrego Valley was considered the most isolated community in San Diego County. In many ways, it still is. Surrounded on three sides by steep mountains and desert hills, with the Borrego Badlands stretching to the east toward the Salton Sea, the Borrego Valley is far from the beaten path.

And yet they came, first the cattlemen, then a scattering of homesteaders. Eventually a community grew up: a place called Borego. By the early 1930s the valley boasted a store and post office, a school, a chamber of commerce and even a local justice of the peace. Soon the State of California began acquiring land in the hills and canyons around the valley to create California's first desert state park. But as late as 1940 there were still no paved roads in the valley, no telephones, no outside electricity.

It was during these formative years that A. A. Burnand, Jr., first came to the Borrego Valley. He was looking for a place to grow winter crops, but he found something more. He found the beauty of the desert, and he found an opportunity. After World War II was over, he decided to share both these things with others. Assembling the necessary land and investors, Burnand announced the birth of a new desert community, Borrego Springs.

Creating a modern community in a remote desert valley was no easy task. The isolation of the Borrego Valley hindered its progress, and yet that same isolation was part of the attraction of Burnand's new community. Others, armed with less determination, or less love for the desert, might have given up, but Burnand and others like him toughed it out and lived to see Borrego Springs grow, survive and thrive.

This is the story of these two communities—the little community of Borego and the modern town of Borrego Springs. It begins around 1910 when the first permanent settlers began to move into the Borrego Valley and continues through the founding of Borrego Springs in 1946, until about 1960. By that time, most of the elements of the modern Borrego Springs were already in place. The growth since then has largely followed the patterns laid down in the early days of the community.

PART I

A PLACE CALLED BOREGO

AN ISOLATED LAND

Long before the modern community of Borrego Springs was founded, there was a place called Borego. Until the 1930s the Borrego Valley was one of the most isolated and least-known parts of San Diego County. Life there in the little homesteader community of Borego was still primitive. As late as 1940 there was not a single paved road in the valley, no electric lines, no telephones. It was San Diego County's last frontier.

To understand Borego's isolation, you have to look at the geography of the area. The Borrego Valley is surrounded on three sides by steep, rocky mountains: the Santa Rosas to the north, the San Ysidros to the west and the Grapevine Hills to the south. To the east, the jumbled mudhills of the Borrego Badlands stretch off towards the Salton Sea.

As late as 1940 there was not a single paved road in the valley, no electric lines, no telephones. It was San Diego County's last frontier.

In the last decades of the nineteenth century, a few cattlemen and sheepherders began driving their stock down to the Borrego Valley for winter grazing. The desert spring in the brushy lower reaches of the valley was a regular watering stop. By the early 1880s that spring was known as Borrego Spring.[1] The name, spelled Borego, first appears on a county map in 1883. It is a misspelling of the Spanish word *borrego* which means a yearling lamb. Colloquially it also means a simpleton or a fool. It has long been assumed that the spring was named because of the Desert Bighorn Sheep that once watered there; but the term borrego usually refers to domestic, not wild, sheep, so perhaps Borrego Spring was named because of the sheepherders who watered their flocks there in the late nineteenth century.

HOMESTEAD DAYS

Almost all the earliest settlers in the Borrego Valley obtained their land by homesteading or other similar government public lands programs. The original Homestead Act of 1862 was amended in 1912, so that most of Borego's homesteaders came in under the new rules. Homesteads were limited to no more than a quarter section, or 160 acres. Any man or unmarried woman over the age of twenty could make a homestead "entry" and file a claim on any unoccupied tract of public land. They were then required to keep a legal residence on their homestead for three years and make various "improvements" including building "a habitable house upon the land" and cultivating at least a portion of the land. Their other option would be to occupy the land for fourteen months and then "commute" their homestead by paying $1.25 an acre for the property. In either case, the final step was to "prove up"

LELAH PORTER

The homestead laws required a "habitable" residence be built on the property; some just barely qualified. This is Douglas Hale's cabin in the northwest part of the valley in 1927.

the claim, by bringing witnesses to swear to the homesteader's occupation and cultivation of the land. Only then would a "patent" (deed) be issued by the government, giving the homesteaders full ownership of the land.[2]

It was not until around 1910 that the first homesteaders began to settle in the Borrego Valley. The Imperial Valley boom—begun by the arrival of irrigation water in 1901—had focused new attention on the desert, and some of that excitement eventually spilled over into Borrego Valley. Among the first homesteaders in the valley were Jack and Katherine French, Bill Schnoke, and Thomas Orland ("Oddie") Fewell and his wife, Estella. The Fewells arrived in 1912 and are said to have been the first couple to live in Borrego Valley. The Frenches dug a shallow well that flowed artesian, and "French's Flowing Well" was a valley landmark for many years.

> **"The greatest advantage the valley offers is its abundant water supply, there being a lake beneath the ground."**
>
> ***San Diego Union***

On January 10, 1913, the *Brawley News* reported:

"Considerable interest is being attached to new development work in the Borego valley, not far from the road between Warner's Hot Springs and Brawley and within a reasonable distance from the Los Angeles highway. The following dispatch in the San Diego Union tells of the good features of the valley, the most serious handicap being the mileage to the railroad.

"That a second Imperial Valley has been discovered in Borego valley is the report of those who have inspected that section with a view of taking up government land. Borego valley lies to the east of Hot Springs mountain, being thirty-nine miles from here, and thirty-nine miles from Mecca, the nearest railroad station on the Southern Pacific railroad. To the nearest point on the San Diego & Arizona railroad is about sixty miles.

"Borego valley comprises about 80,000 acres, all being government land excepting tracts which have been homesteaded. A dozen families have settled there within the last few months.

LELAH PORTER

Judge Kelsey's ranch, 1929. The fields and buildings were typical of many of the valley ranches at the time.

"The greatest advantage the valley offers is its abundant water supply, there being a lake beneath the ground. At several places in the valley water is found four feet below the surface. Drillings in other places have shown that it is not necessary to go deeper than thirty-five feet to get a liberal flow."

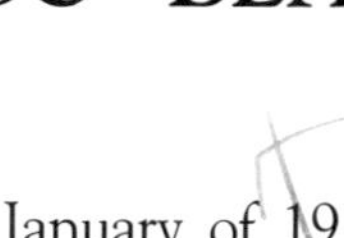

"DOC" BEATY

That same month, January of 1913, Borego's most famous early settler arrived in the valley. Alfred Armstrong "Doc" Beaty (1871-1949) had been a bronc buster, stage driver, resort operator, Imperial Valley boomer and miner. Now he was going to be a desert farmer. With him were his daughter, Fleta, and his wife, Frances. Though only six years old, his daughter never forgot their first glimpse of their new home. They had come down Grapevine Canyon, followed San Felipe Creek down through The Narrows, then turned north over the hills toward the valley.

"I remember we came up the hill and we looked down there, and Borrego Lake [Sink] used to be as white as snow with alkali, and my dad came up to the wagon and he says, 'Well, there it is.' And Mama began to cry; I never will forget it. And she said that, 'You told me it was farming land, what in the world can you farm on that?' "[3]

Doc Beaty, 1944.

Doc's original homestead was located just south of the modern Borrego Springs Airport—a clump of Tamarisk trees still marks the site. But before the year was out he had found some more likely farming land at the mouth of Coyote Canyon, and in November of 1913 he filed a desert claim for an additional 163 acres there.

While Doc was developing the canyon ranch, his family continued to live on their original homestead in the middle of the valley. "We just had a tent with a floor in it that we slept in," Fleta Beaty McCandless recalled, "and we ate and cooked and everything out under the mesquite trees. They were very thick then, and we just cleared a spot for us to live out there."[4]

To make some money, Doc Beaty cut and hauled mesquite wood to sell in Brawley. With a team and a fresno scraper, Doc also did improvement work for other homesteaders. Fleta, who was already old enough to be in school, boarded in Brawley during the school term. With her away and Doc on the job, that left Frances Beaty alone much of the time.

The Beaty Ranch (now Whitaker Horse Camp), 1927.

"I really think more about it now than I did then," her daughter said, "but I don't know how in the world she ever took it. Especially when we first moved out there and lived down there like we did, out in the open and all, when we first homesteaded.

"And Dad would have to go into town. One of his projects was that he got on with Imperial County, and whenever they had a big storm in those days, which they had every summer, there were no bridges, and all those washes would wash out. So they'd get word to Dad to bring his team and wagon and come in. And so he worked in there. So lots of times my mama was there all alone for weeks at a time. I think about it now and I just don't know. Once and a while she'd walk...it was a mile or so down to Frenches', and I can remember even when I was out there with her we'd take off and walk down to Frenches'. But after we moved up above [to the Coyote Canyon ranch], there was a lot more activity there, so she didn't have so much time, except to cook, bless her heart."[5]

After the Beatys proved up on their original homestead in 1917, they moved to the ranch at the mouth of Coyote Canyon. Doc dug an irrigation ditch down from Coyote Creek, built a reservoir and began growing alfalfa. Their first home there was just a ramada. "Then Dad finally put a tent over it to protect us from the wind and all," his daughter recalled. "Later," she said, "we had what we called the cook shack, which was a tent with boards walled up so high and a floor, and slats that we could raise in one area. And then across from it we had another one that they had fixed up to sleep in and visit in or whatever."[6]

> "I remember we came up the hill and we looked down there, and Borrego Lake [Sink] used to be as white as snow with alkali, and my dad came up to the wagon and he says, 'Well, there it is.' And Mama began to cry; I never will forget it. And she said that, 'You told me it was farming land, what in the world can you farm on that?' "
>
> *Fleta Beaty McCandless*

The Beaty Ranch was located right where Whitaker Horse Camp is today in Anza-Borrego Desert State Park. The tent houses are gone, but the Beatys' storage dugout is still standing, and the trace of Doc's ditch is still visible heading up the canyon.

Brawley, in Imperial County, was the supply town for Beaty and most of the other early homesteaders. According to Fleta McCandless, it was a two-and-a-half-day journey there, with wagon and team. They went from water hole to water hole, from Borrego Spring to Barrel Spring (now a part of the Ocotillo Wells State Vehicular Recreation Area) then southeast to Harper's Well, at the junction of San Felipe and Carrizo creeks. From there, they picked up something of a road down to the westside canal, the furthestmost part of the Imperial Valley irrigation system. Then they just followed the canal into Brawley.

In the early 1950s, Frances Beaty recalled that only a handful of homesteaders had already taken up claims in the valley before her arrival in 1913. "In the year 1912, Thomas Fewell and wife built a small house, as they had homesteaded what is now known as the Meyers' place. Next in line was Ed Sims' small cabin. John Dickerson [came] next, his cabin is still standing across from the Ensign date ranch, the one painted white. Then Jack and Mrs.

French had a tent house and drilled the small artesian well that the Campbells still use. William Schnocke was next on their homestead, which was on the land where the trailer camp and [Bud's] Quonset house is.

"These people have all passed away.... Mr. Charles Bemis and son Harold also came in 1912, and in the spring of 1913 brought in a well rig with which they drilled a number of shallow wells. Among them was the well east of the store where the palms are. Mr. Bemis also brought in the first tractor and farm machinery, some of which can still be seen at the Ensign ranch."[7]

By 1916 there were sixteen registered voters in the original Borego Precinct. About that same time, the local homesteaders tried starting a school in the valley. There were only three or four children in the valley then, not enough to justify a school district. But at the suggestion of Charles Bemis and Katherine French, the homesteaders put up the money to hire Mrs. Ruth Brice as a teacher, and classes were held in the Charles Ferguson home for about two months before the idea was abandoned.[8]

The first wave of homesteaders into Borrego Valley reached its peak just before World War I, then followed several years of population decline. In the mid-1920s more and more new homesteaders again began to arrive. Several factors contributed to this next surge of growth. Special homestead laws had made it quicker for returning veterans to file and prove up on a homestead. Other veterans were given state land "script" which could be used to pay for the costs of filing and commuting a homestead. Then in 1922 the first automobile road was opened through Sentenac Canyon, making it easier to reach the valley. The older, rougher Grapevine Canyon road fell into disuse as more and more people began coming down the road from Warners Ranch through the San Felipe Valley. Finally, in 1926, the first deep well in the valley was brought in on the Ensign Ranch, proving that there was an ample supply of water in the aquifer beneath the valley floor.

"The tide is coming in," Borego's correspondent wrote in the *Ramona Sentinel* in June of 1928. "Every day we have some new

McCANDLESS FAMILY

Doc Beaty's home on his original homestead, built with the proceeds of the final sale of his Coyote Canyon ranch in 1931. Quite a step up after years of living in tent houses.

neighbors. With land soaring in price all over Southern California people are steadily coming here to purchase land in our virgin valley. Date palms, grapes, alfalfa, and all kinds of early vegetables thrive here."[9]

Among the many homesteaders coming into the valley in the mid-1920s were Milo and Lelah Porter, who took up a 160-acre homestead in the northwest part of the valley, below the mouth of Henderson Canyon, in 1927. Like a number of the early homesteaders, the Porters didn't plan to settle permanently in the valley; they were going to stay just long enough to get title to their land, then move back to the city. "We were just going to stay fourteen months and then commute our homestead by paying $1.25 an acre," Lelah Porter explains, "...then the Depression came, and we had no jobs to which to go back to, and so we just stayed, because we were getting by down there."[10]

Things were rather primitive on the Porter homestead in the 1920s. Their first home was an eight-by-twelve-foot cabin. A few months later they added a ten-by-twelve-foot addition on each side. The original portion became the kitchen, and one wing served as a bedroom and the other as a living room. Because they were on higher ground it was too deep, and thus too expensive, for the Porters to drill their own well, so they hauled water in a 225-gallon tank on skids, first from French's Flowing Well, then from the Ensigns' well. "The way we lived for the first three years," Porter says, "it was pretty primitive living. But you know, when you're young, it doesn't mean much. You know you're going to make it...you just know it wasn't going to be forever. You just get by."[11]

> "The way we lived for the first three years, it was pretty primitive living. But you know, when you're young, it doesn't mean much. You know you're going to make it...you just know it wasn't going to be forever. You just get by."
>
> *Lelah Porter*

Instead of commuting their homestead after fourteen months, the Porters had to stick it out the full three years, finally proving up in 1930. Then they moved to Lee Bowers' homestead, closer to the center of the valley. Bowers, an absentee owner from Covina, had a good house and a 108-foot drilled well on his ranch. The Porters and their children lived there and raised turkeys until they left the valley for Julian in 1938.

By the end of 1928, "all the suitable homestead lands having been taken up in the Borego district," the valley's brief homesteading boom was at an end.[12] Later that year, the unused veterans' land script was withdrawn, and a number of local homesteaders converted their entries to Desert Land Claims. "This...will be a great boon to well drillers in Borego valley," the *Ramona Sentinel* noted, "as all who prove up under the desert land laws are compelled to develop at least 40 inches of water and cultivate their land."[13]

With all the suitable land taken in the Borrego Valley, some folks decided to try homesteading around Clark Dry Lake. In December, 1929, Borego's correspondent to the *Sentinel* noted, "Where there was but the cattle hut at Clark's well three months ago there are five new homes in the valley, with lumber on the ground for four more."[14]

Two weeks later he wrote: "A rush rivaling the famous Oklahoma land settlers' rush in 1889, only on a smaller scale, is now going on in the Clark valley.... The reason for the present land rush is the fact that Borego valley proper has been settled more or less from a homesteader's standpoint for a great many years, while in the Clark valley the land has only been taken up recently, and every quarter section has a homesteader's cabin on it and the valley is teeming with activity. Wells are being drilled by several of the homesteaders.

"James E. Dennis, for ten years yardmaster for the C.B.&Q. railroad at Galesburg, Illinois, is credited with discovering the rich possibilities of this wonderful little valley and it was his original homestead application which started the present settlement. Among the new settlers who are now living in the valley are Henry Nelson and Fred Robinson...at present employed by the county as road foremen under Supervisor Aul. Miss Drilla DuVall and her brother, Glenn DuVall from St. Louis, Mo., and their uncle, G. A. Rock, Los Angeles city fireman for the past 14 years, have built new houses and are developing their ranches."[15]

But the Clark Valley boom did not last. Jimmie Dennis, "pioneer homesteader of the Clark valley" and a veteran of the Klondike Gold Rush in Alaska, was found dead in August of 1930 along the trail leading to a mining claim he was developing in the Santa Rosa Mountains. The DuValls, joined by their brother, Edward, soon moved into Borrego Valley proper. Others simply moved away. By the end of 1934, Xavier Reynalds was the only homesteader living in Clark Valley.

Some of the settlers did prove up and hold onto their claims. Gilbert Rock (1890-1980) was in the valley as much as his career as a Los Angeles City firefighter would allow. He took a leave of absence to meet his homestead residence requirements and built a home in 1929. He started spending more and more time on his ranch after he retired from the fire department in 1936, and eventually owned about nine hundred acres in the valley.

THE ENSIGN RANCH

The Ensign Ranch was the first large-scale farming operation in the Borrego Valley. O. H. Ensign (1863-1935), a Los Angeles carburetor manufacturer and former United States Bureau of Reclamation engineer, began visiting the valley around 1920, after his son, Roy, had married Charles Bemis' daughter, Muriel. In 1926, Ensign began buying land in Section nine in the center of the valley (where Club Circle is today), and put in the first deep well in the valley, a 160-footer that could produce up to 1,000 gallons a minute. Two more deep wells were drilled in 1932 and 1945. Without access to outside electricity, the pumps had to be run by gasoline or diesel generators, which thumped away twenty-four hours a day.

The first cash crop on the Ensign Ranch was alfalfa. By 1928 Ensign had two hundred acres under irrigation, and in 1929 the *Ramona Sentinel* reported, "A crop of alfalfa hay is mowed and stacked every month on the Ensign ranch. The last crop made a growth of 30 inches in 30 days."[16] Sweet potatoes, watermelons, wheat, barley and milo maize were also grown on the ranch in the years to come.

HAROLD ENSIGN

The Ensign Ranch, circa 1930, showing the original ranch house on the left and the new manager's house on the right. Between them are the well and pump house.

But the Ensign Ranch's most famous crop was dates. The first date palms were planted on the ranch in 1927 and 1928, set out in a one-and-a-half-acre nursery. To combat the disease pests that infest date orchards worldwide, the date shoots destined for Borego were baked for forty-eight hours at 165 degrees. The process killed many of the shoots, but the blackened stumps that survived were pest-free, and Borego's isolation kept them that way.

Well-drilling on the Ensign Ranch in the late 1920s. Notice the steam-powered engine with its drive belts.

O. H. Ensign visits the start of his date grove in the early 1930s.

In 1933 the trees were replanted in an eight-acre orchard. The palms were "planted as a harem, the groves having about one male tree for every forty-five female trees per acre."[17] The female palms were capable of producing about 250 pounds of dates a year. The Ensigns continued to enlarge their date orchard, first to twenty, and finally to thirty-five acres. The trees take many years to mature. It was not until 1939 that the first small commercial harvest was made. In 1942, forty thousand pounds of Ensign dates were sold at about forty cents a pound. Two years later the Ensigns shipped sixty thousand pounds of dates from thirteen producing acres.

In 1949 the Ensigns built a date shop along Borrego Valley Road, but there was not enough retail business to justify its continuing operation. Most of the Ensign dates were trucked to the Coachella Valley and marketed through local wholesalers there. The date shop building was later taken over by the Borrego Springs Park Community Services District and still stands on Borrego Valley Road.

Beginning in 1929, the Ensigns also raised hogs on the ranch, which were allowed to graze in the date orchard, where, "besides keeping the ground clear of weeds, [they] aid in fertilizing the soil."[18] Like a number of Borego ranchers, the Ensigns also went into the turkey business in the 1930s, and by the middle of the decade were raising thousands of "poults" each year.

HAROLD ENSIGN

Roy Ensign working on the electrical plant on the Ensign Ranch.

HAROLD ENSIGN

E. D. Small, the foreman of the Ensign Ranch, inspecting one of their hogs, circa 1930.

In 1930, Ensign's son, Roy, began developing his own alfalfa and turkey ranch north of his father's ranch. Both ranches were enlarged over the years, and after O. H. Ensign died in 1935 they were combined, and Roy and his brother, Paul, took over a 1,040-acre spread.

The Ensigns continued to add new enterprises on the ranch. In 1929, government agricultural officials made the first experimental cotton plantings in the valley on the O. H. Ensign Ranch. In 1936, Harold Bemis brought in the equipment and the first thirty-four guernsey cows as the start of a dairy herd on Roy's ranch.

The headquarters on the Ensign Ranch in the 1940s.

The day-to-day operation of the Ensign ranches was always under the charge of resident managers. The O. H. Ensign Ranch was originally run by E. D. Small and his sons Reg and Melbourne, who was better known as Buster. Managing the most successful ranch in the valley did have its perks. In 1929 the *Ramona Sentinel* reported, "A new modern four-room house is nearing completion on the Ensign ranch. It will have a shower and tub bath, electric lights, cellar and screen porch. Mr. Small and son will live in the house."[19] The Smalls ran the ranch until 1933. Lewis Smith was manager in 1935 and 1936.

J. A. Kelsey, who had an adjoining homestead in Section four, served as Roy Ensign's first manager. Al Teagarden was manager by 1933, and, after he resigned in 1935, Paul Stewart took over. When the two Ensign ranches were combined around 1937, Harold Bemis seems to have served briefly as manager. Tom Davis came to work on the combined ranch around 1939, and shortly after 1940 was promoted to manager. He stayed on until the family sold the ranch in the 1950s.

The Ensign Ranch was not always profitable for the family, but they stuck with it through good years and bad for almost four decades. The Ensigns proved that large-scale agriculture was possible in the valley and helped to attract many other settlers to the desert.

THE DE ANZA RANCH

The other prize ranch in the valley was Doc Beaty's place at the mouth of Coyote Canyon, irrigated by the waters of Coyote Creek. As interest in the valley grew in the late 1920s, Doc tried selling it to outside investors several times, the first in 1927, but the deals all fell through for one reason or another. In 1929-30 the Felicita Land and Water Company, a group of Los Angeles County investors, was running the ranch, which they renamed the Thousand Palms Ranch. Rex Odell was their foreman, and the ubiquitous Harry Woods was their sales manager. Finally, in 1931, Doc sold the place once and for all to a group of "Santa Monica capitalists."

Armed with the cash from the sale, Doc "got a brain-storm that he wanted to put pecans in and raise pecans of all things," his daughter, Fleta, recalled. Moving back to his original homestead, Doc had one well drilled, then another, following his final sale of the ranch in 1931. A year later, he planted twenty acres of pecan trees, "and not a one of them lived!" his daughter said.[20] After the pecan deba-

BORREGO SUN

A beautiful panorama of the De Anza Ranch, circa 1940, showing the reservoir and the planted fields where Whitaker Horse Camp is now located. The white house was built by Albert Ahern; A. A. Burnand's ranch house sits just to the right. Both houses still stand.

WHITAKER

cle, Doc Beaty went back to growing alfalfa and row crops such as onions on his valley homestead. He also tried cabbages one year—another failure.

Also with the money from the sale of the canyon ranch, he built a permanent home for himself. According to his grandson and namesake, former United States Congressman Al McCandless: "The house itself was just basic shelter by today's standards, but after a canvas house it was a palace. It had a corrugated steel roof, a front porch, an underground cellar that served as a refrigerator, that huge stone fireplace in the living room, two bedrooms and a utility room, a kitchen and a two-holer out back."[21]

> **"The house itself was just basic shelter by today's standards, but after a canvas house it was a palace."**
>
> *Al McCandless*
> *Doc Beaty's grandson*

Doc lived there until his death in 1949. His cherished fireplace eventually became a poolside barbecue when the Molino Verde Motel was built on the site in the 1950s. It was finally torn down around 1988.

The new owners of the Thousand Palms Ranch leased the property to John Freeman, a Brawley farmer, who planted tomatoes and other vegetables alongside Doc's alfalfa fields. In 1933 developer Dana Burks bought the place and leased it to Ray Kanemaru, who grew "winter peas, winter tomatoes, and Kentucky Wonder beans."[22] Burks again renamed the ranch, dubbing it the Rancho de Anza. Kanemaru stayed on when Burks sold the ranch to Albert Ahern and Donald Armstrong in 1934. Ahern, a retired Santa Monica furrier, built a house on the ranch, which still stands. Armstrong's son, Donald, served as the "warden" for the new Borego Palms State Park in the winter of 1934-35.

Early in 1936 Ahern acquired a new partner, A. A. Burnand, Jr., a grape grower from California's Central Valley. In 1937 Burnand planted 120 acres of Thompson Seedless grapes on the ranch. The vineyard never produced a paying crop, but Burnand stuck with it, eventually buying out his partners and going on to found the modern community of Borrego Springs.

AGRICULTURE

Just as other settlers had done in the Imperial and Coachella valleys, Borego's early settlers hoped to make the desert bloom. Along the way, they experimented with all sorts of crops. Some proved successful; most were failures.

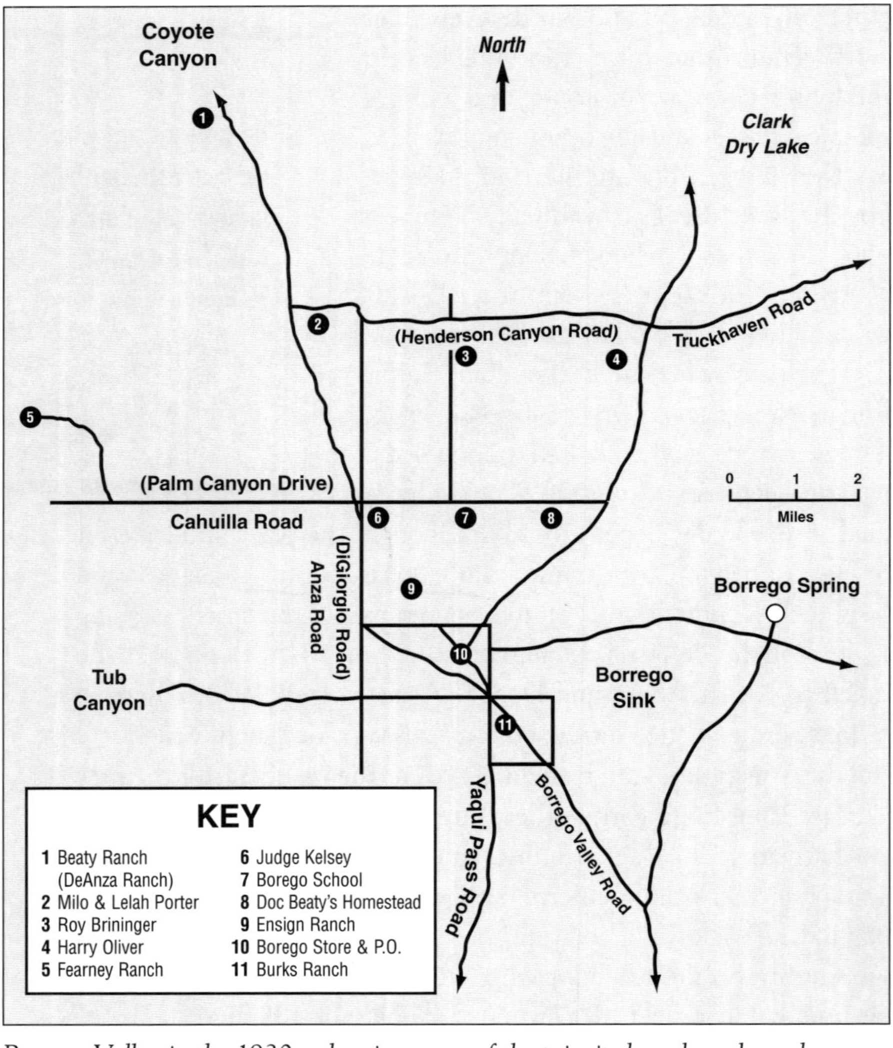

Borrego Valley in the 1930s, showing some of the principal roads and ranches.

The valley's first cash crop was alfalfa. Doc Beaty was selling alfalfa in Imperial Valley from his Coyote Canyon Ranch as far back as the 'teens, and by 1921 had twenty-six irrigated acres. Alfalfa was also the first cash crop on the Ensign Ranch. By 1931 Ensign alfalfa was selling at eighteen dollars a ton. The Ensigns were also the major local growers of other grain crops, including wheat and barley.

HAROLD ENSIGN

Cutting alfalfa on the Ensign Ranch, 1929.

HAROLD ENSIGN

Cattle grazing on the alfalfa stubble on the Ensign Ranch in the 1940s.

Various row crops were tried in the valley, including corn, asparagus, onions, sweet potatoes, milo maize, cabbage and watermelons. Tom Miller grew lettuce, while others tried cucumbers, bell peppers, summer squash, winter peas, Irish potatoes, black-eyed beans, eggplants and, of course, Doc Beaty's pecans. Foreshadowing the Fortiners by a dozen years, Roy Brininger even planted a few gladiola bulbs in 1933. No one knew for sure just which crops would both flourish and prove profitable. The only way to find out was to give them a try.

Judge Joseph Kelsey was one of the most active experimenters, growing crops on his own homestead and the adjoining Ensign Ranch. Over the years, Kelsey cultivated cantaloupes, pineapples, papayas, sweet potatoes, lemons, oranges, grapefruit, figs, apricots, onions, corn, milo maize, cabbage, garlic and Virginia peanuts, "which seem to do exceptionally well in the Borego Valley." Judge Kelsey raised a field of asparagus on the

Early-day plowing on the Ensign Ranch.

Ensign Ranch in 1930, and sweet potatoes were doing well on the Beaty Ranch that same spring. In 1933 he was planning "five acres of apricots, two acres of Thompson Seedless and Early Kandahar grapes, a mixed assortment of fruit trees, and a half acre of Youngberries"[23]

With support from government agricultural officials, the Ensigns began experimenting with cotton in 1929. Dana Burks also had an experimental planting in 1933. In 1937, sixty acres of cotton was raised on the Ensign Ranch and hauled down to a gin in Imperial Valley.

Albin Laag, a 'teens homesteader, is said to have made an unsuccessful grape planting on his place south of the Borrego Sink, before World War I. Claude Garner was one of the next to plant grape vines in the valley, bringing in 125,000 cuttings in 1928. Dana Burks put in a fifteen-acre vineyard of assorted varieties in 1933. Roy Brininger was shipping Thompson Seedless by 1936. As of 1937, there were nearly 150 acres of Thompson Seedless vines in the valley, including the 120 acres just planted on the DeAnza Ranch by A. A. Burnand.

The first citrus plantings in the valley began around 1930. Oranges, lemons, limes, grapefruit and tangelos were planted, with Roy Brininger's trees proving the most successful. Oddie Fewell had the first two date palms in the valley, planted in 1917. Later the Ensign Ranch would become the valley's biggest grower.

Tomatoes were one of the early successes. They were probably the only crop, except for alfalfa, that was shipped every season throughout the 1930s. Fred Lanz, who came to Borego in 1927, was known as the valley's "Tomato King." His ranch was at the mouth of Tub Canyon. Other early commercial growers included Roy Brininger, Frank Scheck, the Fearney brothers, and Dana Burks. Edward Riverall had twenty-five acres of tomatoes on his ranch, now the site of the DeAnza Country Club, in 1934. In February, 1936, Lanz was shipping about forty lugs a week. By April, Brininger was shipping 100 lugs a day and hoped to harvest 5,000 lugs that season.

LELAH PORTER

Mervyn and Milene Porter and a visiting friend check out the Porters' turkey flock in the mid-1930s.

During the 1930s, some of the ranchers would lease their fields to Japanese farmers from Imperial Valley who planted various row crops, especially tomatoes. Joe Kodama began growing tomatoes and eggplants on the Brininger Ranch in 1934 and stayed in the valley for the rest of the decade. He harvested a crop of tomatoes on the DeAnza Ranch in the spring of 1936, then planted another crop on the Neel Ranch that same summer. Ray Kanemaru raised tomatoes on the DeAnza Ranch in the mid-1930s and managed the ranch for Ahern and Armstrong in 1935.[24]

Also in the 1930s, poultry raising gained popularity on the desert. Judge Kelsey was raising turkeys by 1929. Roy Brininger soon followed. By 1931 there were twelve hundred birds on the Ensign Ranch, two hundred at Brininger's, and Victor Nason had 250. Milo Porter kept chickens on the Bowers Ranch in 1933-34, but later switched to turkeys. Over in Clark Valley, Xavier Reynolds even made a stab at raising ducks. But turkeys proved most successful. By 1935 there were three thousand birds on the O. H. Ensign Ranch, and his son, Roy, had two thousand more. William Morton got into turkeys in 1936 and soon had one thousand birds. Worth Toner's turkey ranch on the north side of the highway at Dry Lake (Ocotillo Wells) was also well known in the mid-1930s.

> **"When you had one good year in Borrego Valley, the flowers were good and all that, you had about thirteen that weren't so good."**
>
> ***Lester Reed***

The Ensigns began raising hogs around 1929. Medford Courtney seems to have been the only other rancher to try to follow suit. Pioneer homesteader Bill Schnocke was raising goats in the winter of 1920-21 and also worked with some of the cattlemen who still grazed their herds in the valley. Frank Clark and the Reed brothers, Lester, Gib and Zeke, still brought cattle down from Anza via Coyote Canyon almost every winter. Lester Reed used to chuckle about the cattle they fattened on Borrego's now-famous wildflowers, but, he admitted, "When you had one good year in Borrego Valley, the flowers were good and all that, you had about thirteen that weren't so good."[25] In the 1920s, Frank Clark bought eighty acres in the northeast part of the valley where he established a permanent cattle camp. Sometime before, an exploratory oil well had been put down on the property, which turned out to be a water well instead. Clark continued to run cattle in the valley well into the 1930s.

Albert Teagarden, the manager of the Roy Ensign Ranch, brought the first dairy cattle to the valley in 1933, "another industry badly needed in Borego Valley," the *Ramona Sentinel* noted. "There has always been a shortage of good fresh milk."[26] In 1936, new manager Harold Bemis put the Ensign Ranch into the dairy business on a commercial basis, bringing in thirty-four Guernsey cows, milking machines and a cream separator. The Ensigns continued their dairy operation until 1946.

THE BOREGO STORE AND POST OFFICE

On March 1, 1928, Borego opened its own post office, with Eslie Wynn as its first postmaster.[27] His homestead was strategically located along the south side of the valley, very near to where the old hogback road from The Narrows came down into the valley. He built a solid, half-rock home and had a hand-dug well that went down just twelve feet to good water. The original post office was located in his home. In 1928 he installed a gas pump out front and opened the valley's first gas station. In 1929 he had a new building built across from his home and moved the post office there. That September he opened the valley's first grocery store.

FLETA BEATY MCCANDLESS

Eslie Wynn, posing in the doorway for the new Borego Post Office, 1928.

Wynn's store and post office was as much of a downtown as Borego ever had. In 1929 a branch of the San Diego County Library opened there. In 1933 Wynn added an auto garage, apparently run by James Thomson. All these buildings still stand along the north side of Rango Way on Fleetwood Garner's "Old Borego" ranch.

Borego's mail came down by truck from Julian, first two, and then three days a week. Henry Nelson was the first to haul the mail, then Milo Porter got the contract. "He got sixty dollars a month," his widow, Lelah, says, "and furnished his own transportation and his own gasoline." He would also haul passengers or buy groceries, feed and other necessities for local homesteaders while in town.

BORREGO SUN

Eddie DuVall's Borego Valley store and post office, 1938.

Porter carried the mail for nearly two years, 1928 to 1930. His biggest adventure came in January of 1930, when a freak snow storm blanketed the desert. Porter, with fourteen-year-old Edward Butz riding passenger, got bogged down on the Banner Grade, "where he and Mr. Butz were forced to abandon the car to the storm and continue the journey on foot, with the mail sacks on their backs," the *Ramona Sentinel* reported.

"Through the blinding storm they trudged, the cold becoming more intense with each step, fighting the drowsy pangs of frost-bite, until Butz finally became so drowsy that he declared that he could go no further, and he lay down on the doorstep of an abandoned cabin and Mr. Porter continued his way through the snowdrifts until he reached the county road camp [below Julian] where he explained his dilemma to Mr. Beardsley and the boys there. Hastily they got some mules together and rode back down the grade to where Butz was found sleeping where Mr. Porter had left him. To the nearness of the road camp and the kindness of the boys who work there, Mr. Butz owes being awakened from the sleep of the frost-bitten."[28]

Porter and Butz spent the night at the road camp and made it into Julian the next day. Meanwhile, back in Borego, when Milo didn't come home that night, Lelah Porter was growing frantic. Two of the workmen from the Beaty Ranch showed up with a truck, and Lelah set off with them to look for her husband. They made it as far as the prison camp at Tamarisk Grove, where one of the officials told Lelah, "Oh yeah, we got word he got along up there and everything is all right." It was an out-and-out lie, but it kept Lelah from pushing on into the storm. "What difference did it make," he later told her, "you couldn't have done anything anyway." "But I'd have done something," she says seventy years later, "I would have walked!"[29]

Fred Robinson drove the mail from July, 1930, until February, 1932, when he gave up the contract to go to work for the county road department. When Robinson left, Eslie Wynn decided he would rather haul the mail than sort it, and secured the mail route contract. Because he could not hold both government positions, Wynn stepped down as postmaster on March 1, 1932, and mechanic James Thomson took over the job.

One day in January, 1935, Wynn drove up to the post office with the day's mail. Lelah Porter recalls what happened next: "People

LELAH PORTER

Lelah and Milo Porter (couple at right) lean against the truck Milo used to haul the mail for Borego, circa 1930.

would just congregate down at the post office when the mail came in about four o'clock. It was a meeting place, and you'd get to see everybody. So we were down there...[and] Wynn came in and took the mail on in, and then he came out and said 'Milo, I want you to go with me as a witness. These fellows rented some burros from me and they never paid me...' So Milo got in his car with him and went on over. And Milo told me he barely got there when old Wynn just let go: 'You so-and-so, why haven't you paid me?' And there were two men, and they of course started hitting back. And Milo wasn't a very big man...but he said, 'I got between 'em finally and I told Wynn that wasn't the way to handle things. If he wanted to sue them, sue 'em, but don't start anything.' He said, 'I got 'em separated' and he got Wynn back in the car and when he [Wynn] had driven about half-way back to the post office, he just...[had a seizure]. Milo said, 'I got my foot on the brake and got the car stopped...and pushed him over on the passenger side and brought him on to the post office.' He was gone, he was dead."[30]

To fill the void created by Wynn's death, Milo Porter applied for and again was given the mail contract, which ran until July, 1938.

James Thomson left the valley for Los Angeles in the summer of 1934, and Clark Valley homesteader Glenn DuVall became Borego's postmaster. After Wynn's death, DuVall and his brother, Edward, bought Wynn's old store. In 1936, Eddie DuVall (1905-1973) took over the store and the postmastership. His son, Denny, recalls that his father had a '35 Ford with a trailer, that he would take to San Diego and load up with groceries. "He'd come back and the rear bumper would be about six inches off the ground!"[31]

Eddie DuVall continued to run his Borego Valley Store (never adding a second "r"), into the 1950s. The Borego Post Office survived until July 31, 1940, when it was discontinued, along with a number of other smaller post offices. For the next few years, homesteaders' mail was delivered from Julian via the Borego Star Route, with Al Mathes doing the driving. It was not until 1949 that the Borrego Springs Post Office opened.

THE BOREGO SCHOOL

Another example of Borego's growing civic identity, and population, was the Borego School, which opened in 1928. Doc Beaty, Margaret Disney and others lobbied hard in San Diego to convince the County Superintendent of Schools, Ada York, that the valley was ready for its own school district. But York was hesitant. "She hated to bring in a school," says Disney's daughter, Margaret Boch, "because she said they'd be there a couple of years and then close."[32] But Doc and the others persisted, and York finally gave in and authorized the creation of an "emergency" Borego School District; emergency in the sense that all the formal steps for creating a school district were not taken. York simply declared Borego a school district and authorized the funds to hire a teacher.

The first classes were held on September 20, 1928, in Harold Bemis' cabin on the south side of the valley, about a mile east of the store. Addie Woolsey was the first teacher, and there were twenty-two students. "No one ever weathered greater hardships than did this little lady," Mrs. Herbert LaNiece later recalled.[33] The community also elected its first temporary school board, consisting of Mrs.

SAN DIEGO NATURAL HISTORY MUSEUM

The Borego School, 1931.

Disney, Harold Bemis and Mrs. Leo Klingel, whose husband was one of the World War I vets who homesteaded in the valley.

The school held its first Christmas program that December, which was a success despite rather windy weather. The children ate "baked beans and burro," and Miss Woolsey was presented with "a beautifully tanned burro-skin rug."[34]

burro?

Margaret (Disney) Boch was one of Borego's first four eighth-grade graduates at the end of that first school year. "One of the few social events [in 1929] was my graduation," she recalls. "I think the whole valley was there." Margaret went on to Julian Union High School, boarding with the principal and graduating with the class of 1934. Her parents later moved to Julian and ran a dormitory for students from Borego and other outlying districts who came in to go to high school. Addie Woolsey taught in Borego for two years, then was followed in 1930-31 by Ruth West.

Throughout 1929 and 1930, local residents continued to push for the creation of a permanent school district in the valley, and, after "a spirited discussion" at a public meeting in January, 1931, Ada York agreed to make the necessary recommendation to the County Board of Supervisors. The Borego School District was finally officially created on July 1, 1931. Doc Beaty, Elwin D. Small and Milo Porter were appointed as the first, interim Board of Trustees. Later that year local voters elected Tom Miller, Drilla DuVall (later Mrs. Reg Small) and Arvena Carsey (later Mrs. J. A. Kelsey).

The first teacher hired by the new school district was Emalyn Holland, who had a homestead in the valley. Holland proved popular with parents and students alike. After one year at the Borego School, she moved over to the Dry Lake School at Little Borrego (which had opened in 1926), and taught there until the school closed in 1935. Holland then returned to Borego and was the valley's teacher until 1941.

The new district also started "bus" service in 1931, courtesy of an old Cadillac sedan driven by Glenn DuVall. When the district ran short of funds to pay him, Doc Beaty made up the difference out of his own pocket. In November, 1931, some of the ladies of the valley formed a sewing circle to piece a quilt that was raffled off on New Year's Eve to raise money for the school bus. The sewing circle grew into the Borego P.T.A. in 1932.

In 1933-34 there was a push to move the school from the Bemis house to a more central location. J. A. Kelsey, Borego's representative on the Julian Union High School board, complained in his Borego column in the *Ramona Sentinel*: "It is about time for the people of Borego Valley to wake up and think about owning their own school house. The house now used for school purposes is located in the coldest and most disagreeable part of the Valley, in winter. All the water supply has to be hauled, as it was 50 years ago. The writer is of the opinion that our children of the rural districts are entitled to all the modern conveniences as well as the city children."[35]

The new district also started "bus" service in 1931, courtesy of an old Cadillac sedan driven by Glenn DuVall. When the district ran short of funds to pay him, Doc Beaty made up the difference out of his own pocket.

Everyone seemed to agree that a new schoolhouse was needed, but just where to put it was still an open question. Several local landowners offered property to the district. Kelsey was as contemptuous of some of the proposed sites as he was towards the old Bemis place. "Eslie Wynn's mud flats and the windswept plains of Estabrook are out of the question," he wrote. The site must be "near geographical center of valley."[36]

Finally, local developer Dana Burks stepped forward to offer five acres of land along "Cahuilla Road" (as Palm Canyon Drive was then known), at what is still the site of the Borrego Elementary School today. By public vote, the people of the valley decided to accept his offer, but somewhere along the way, Burks' gift grew. "Dana Burks offered this land where the grammar school is now," Lelah Porter recalls, "and he gave us supposedly five acres, but he forgot the last quarter [section in the legal description]. I don't know whether intentionally or unintentionally, so we got twenty acres instead of five acres. Well, at that time land was so cheap that he didn't care."[37]

A $6,000 bond election to pay for a new schoolhouse was held in July of 1934, but failed. Without funds to build a new school, the trustees bought an old homestead cabin, built by Kelsey Hall in 1927, and moved it to the new site with the help of the crew from the county road camp. Classes began on the present site in November of 1934; the average attendance was just six children in all eight grades.

> **"After the house was moved on the present school site the people in the community all got busy raising money by quilt raffles, dances, and donations for the school."**
>
> ***Milo Porter***

In the winter of 1935-36, Hall's old cabin was enlarged and improved, and a cafeteria was added. During the construction, classes were held in Dana Burks' adobe (now the entrance to La Casa del Zorro). Milo Porter later recalled: "After the house was moved on the present school site the people in the community all got busy raising money by quilt raffles, dances, and donations for the school. The district had some money, but we needed so much more to bring the school building up comparable to other small schools in the district.

"We bought a Bell and Howell movie projector, and the representatives of the Bell and Howell company wired the schoolhouse for electricity. We had bought a light plant which was placed in the well house. The water tank was bought and moved from what was known at the time as the Riverall Ranch on the west side of the valley near Palm Canyon Wash. Also at this time a cafeteria room was built on to the new school building by George W. Crowley and Asa Hare. Upon the completion of this addition the mothers of the valley took turns serving dinners to the children in school.... As we remember it, the mothers took advantage of any surplus food offered by the government, and, to make up the difference in cost, each child was charged fifteen cents a week, and it was later raised to twenty-five cents a week. I might add that that was in the days when thirty-five cents per hour was fair wages. The cafeteria was still operating in 1938 when we left the valley."[38]

LELAH PORTER

The Borego School and the entire student body, 1936. Shown, left to right, are: (front row) Mervyn Porter, one of the Pittman boys, Milene Porter, Betty Carsey, Jimmy Morton, Michael Simon and Richard Butz; (back row) George Pratt, Donald Pratt, George (Kodama?), their teacher, Emalyn Holland, Harold Pittman and Herman Pittman.

The new electrified schoolhouse also doubled as a community center for evening meetings, dinners and dances. Attendance in the district dropped so low during World War II that the school was closed for one year, 1943-44, but then it reopened and has been active ever since. Classes were held in the old building until 1950, and then it served as the custodian's residence. In 1954 the district offered the old building for sale, but there were no takers. In 1958 the district ordered it demolished, but Lou Hahne bought it instead and had it moved to his service station for a parts building. Sadly, the old building was destroyed by fire in 1994.

VOTING PRECINCT AND TOWNSHIP

The original Borego Precinct had long since lapsed by 1928 when, again with Doc Beaty's support, Borego once again became a separate voting precinct. Lelah Porter got swept up into Doc's scheming. "He came to me one day and he said, 'I have a Republican and a Democrat and a Prohibitionist,' he said, 'and if you'll register as a Socialist I'll put you on the election board.' Well, you know, I was almost twenty-two, but I had never registered to vote because at that time the age limit was twenty-one. And, I went home and told my dad that I had registered as a Socialist and he hit the ceiling! He said, 'You go down there and you register Republican. I won't have a daughter of mine being a Socialist!' Well I didn't even know what a Socialist was, but I went through that election, then I re-registered after that election. But I was on the first election board down there with Doc Beaty and Mrs. Rice...and Eslie Wynn."[39]

> **"Borego township, strangely enough, has no commercial center. There is no 'town' site, no crossroads, no centralized settlement. It's spread over the valley and is typical desert country. However, big things are happening to Borego Valley in small ways."**
>
> ***San Diego Union***

In 1930 the San Diego County Board of Supervisors also authorized a Borego Judicial Township. Its boundaries included what is now Ocotillo Wells and the Tamarisk Grove area. The township officially came into existence on February 4, 1931, with Joseph A. Kelsey as justice of the peace and Milo Porter as constable. "Their jurisdiction covers much space and little population," the *San Diego Union* reported. "Borego township has a population of about 300, with 148 registered voters. The center of the township is 10 miles north of the Julian-Kane Springs road, and about 38 miles from Julian.

"Borego township, strangely enough, has no commercial center. There is no 'town' site, no crossroads, no centralized settlement. It's spread over the valley and is typical desert country. However, big things are happening to Borego Valley in small ways. It is a township, with a constable and justice of [the] peace who admit they will have little to do. Both Kelsey and Porter were appointed by the board of supervisors to serve until January 1, 1932."[40]

Porter was Borego's only constable. In 1932 a new County Charter was enacted, and all the township constables were replaced with deputy sheriffs. Once again, Porter retained the job, serving until 1935, when Bill Morton took over. Later, Eddie DuVall served as Borego's deputy sheriff for fourteen years.[41]

Judge Kelsey continued as justice of the peace until his death in 1937. His widow, Arvena, filled the post unofficially for the next few months before moving out of the valley in the summer of 1938, but it seems she never heard a single case. In the November election that year two write-in candidates, Charles Fearney and Alex MacLeod, tied for the job, seventeen votes apiece. A run-off election was set for January 24, 1939, when thirty-eight of Borego's forty-nine registered voters turned up at the polls and elected Fearney, twenty-one to seventeen.

CIVIC ORGANIZATIONS

The Borego Valley's first community organization was the Borego Boosters Club, which was formed in December, 1928. Ensign Ranch manager E. D. Small served as its first chairman. The Boosters started off with several goals: better roads into the valley,

DEMARAIS COLLECTION - SAN DIEGO HISTORICAL SOCIETY RESEARCH ARCHIVES

A promotional brochure published by the Borego Valley Chamber of Commerce in 1933.

better publicity about the valley and a community hall for the valley.

Plans for a community building were developed during 1929. In the meantime, the Boosters usually met at developer G. M. Jones' home near the present site of Christmas Circle. Before the year was out it was decided to incorporate the group formally as the Borego Valley Chamber of Commerce. The organizational meeting was held on December 12, 1929, and then that Saturday, "a great jollification meeting, supper and dance was held which lasted until the wee hours of Sunday morning. Games were played, together with dancing by the younger set, followed by a big supper prepared by the ladies of the valley."[42]

The first officers of the new chamber of commerce were Rex Odell, president; Lloyd Kelsey, vice president; Lelah Porter, treasurer; and Gladys Osborne, secretary; with Doc Beaty, F. B. Osborne, Milo Porter, Nora Carpenter and Judge Kelsey filling out the board of directors. Milo Porter became president in July, 1930, and served until early 1932.

Borego's community building was never built, but in 1931, with financial support from the county, the chamber published a promotional brochure, inviting outlanders to "LIVE! in Borego Valley California's Wonderland."

The brochure touted Borego's "scenic wonders," its "early garden stuffs, such as cucumbers, melons and tomatoes" and the eleven cuttings of alfalfa some ranchers were harvesting each year; its "interesting and profitable" hog industry; its turkeys; its "experimental" dates and other "promising" crops; its "inextinguishable" water supply; and even its "optimistic" oil possibilities. "Borego climatic conditions are very favorable as a health resort," the brochure promised, "particularly in such illnesses as asthma, pleurisy, bronchitis, tuberculosis, etc. The winters are exceptionally mild and pleasant and because of the low humidity the summer heat is not oppressive."[43]

The Borego Valley Chamber of Commerce remained active until at least 1938, but seems to have faded away before World War II.

Many of the 1920s homesteaders in Borego were World War I veterans, since special laws made it much easier for them to prove up a homestead. In 1931 they organized a local branch of the American Legion, under the sponsorship of the Ramona Legion Post, where many of them were members. The Borego group was still meeting in the winter of 1934-35, but later lapsed.

> **"One year, I know, we had it [Easter Sunrise Service] up on Sleepy Hollow... And cold! If ever 'the sands of the desert grew cold'...I was never so cold in all my life."**
>
> *Lelah Porter*

While Borego never had a church, "We always had a Sunday School down there in Borego," says Lelah Porter, "seems like from the very beginning when we first went in. I suppose Milo and I along with a bunch of other people just decided we'd have a Sunday School. And we always had an Easter Sunrise Service. Even if we danced all night we'd still have an Easter Sunrise Service. One year, I know, we had it up on Sleepy Hollow...near the Disney place. And cold! If ever 'the sands of the desert grew cold'...I was never so cold in all my life."[44]

Sunday School classes were underway as early as 1928, and Easter Sunrise was being celebrated by 1930. A more formal Union Sunday School was organized in April of 1930, with Margaret Disney as superintendent. Visiting ministers also held Sunday Services in the valley from time to time during the winter months, usually in the schoolhouse.

BOREGO CIRCA 1930

Despite the beginnings of the Depression, Borego entered the 1930s with great hope for the future. On January 1, 1931, the *San Diego Union* published a detailed review of local developments:

Borego Valley Residents Make Many Improvements

"Developments have been proceeding at a rapid rate in Borego valley in the northern part of San Diego county, adjacent to the Imperial county line, that give promise of this fertile valley eventually becoming the breadbasket of San Diego.... The Borego Valley Growers, Inc., a syndicate of Hollywood motion picture directors, has spent several thousand dollars in developing a fine property in the eastern section of the valley. A fine well has been drilled which produces in excess of 100 miner's inches of water at a lift of about 80 feet. It is planned to develop this property into a colony of winter homes for filmland folk and plant grapefruit, dates, alfalfa and figs. Harry Oliver, a member of the syndicate, has completed a fine new adobe residence and several more of these structures are contemplated for erection this year."

[Borego's Hollywood connection were not all directors. Ferd Sersen was a "scenic director" for Fox. His ranch was managed by his brother-in-law, Medford Courtney. Albert Vansco was a set builder. Paul Widlicska was another Hollywood homesteader, but the best-known was Harry Oliver (1888-1973), an art director at Fox. He became fascinated with the legends and lore of the Borrego Desert and, in 1938, published *Desert Rough Cuts: A Haywire History of the Borego Valley*, a fanciful piece that foreshadowed his famous *Desert Rat Scrapbook* which began publication in 1946. Oliver also declared himself the press agent for Peg Leg Smith, the nineteenth century trapper who had supposedly found, then lost, a mammoth gold deposit somewhere on the desert. In 1948 Oliver founded the Peg Leg Smith Liars Contest, which despite a hiatus in the '60s and early

'70s, is still held annually. His adobe home, built in 1930, still stands, not far from the site of the contest, the Peg Leg Smith Monument, along county road S-22.]

"Roy Brininger is preparing to have drilled for him a 300-foot well on his ranch in the center of the valley and has engaged the Taylor Brothers of Coachella, pioneer well drillers of the desert, for this undertaking. Brininger has associated with him Wilbur Hutchinson of Chicago, and they plan to raise turkeys."

LELAH PORTER

Billy Crowley poses with some of the desert artifacts on the Brininger Ranch in the early 1930s. A number of the early settlers collected ollas and other Indian relics.

[Brininger's ranch was one of the showplaces of the valley in the 1930s. He came from Culver City in the late '20s and filed a homestead at the upper end of the valley, near what is now the southeast corner of DiGiorgio and Henderson Canyon roads. Besides raising turkeys, he grew various crops including tomatoes and some experimental plantings of grapes and citrus. The *San Diego Union* (March 19, 1933) reported that Brininger had "a 20-acre patch which supports some 62,000 cuttings of different varieties of vine, truck and orchard crops set out for next year's planting." Brininger died early in 1937 at the age of 54.]

"At the 1000 Palms Ranch [the old Beaty place] at the head of the valley there is a development project in the making, with a view to harnessing the Coyote Creek and placing this water on several thousand acres of fertile land.

"Thomas Miller, World War I veteran and former resident of San Diego, is developing water on his ranch near Borego springs and plans an extensive development."

[Tom Miller took up a homestead about a mile north of the Borego store around 1926. He was in the valley throughout most of the rest of the 1930s, serving as local deputy sheriff, as a member of the school board from 1931-33, and as vice president of the chamber of commerce.]

"F. B. Osborne has developed a small well upon his property and has constructed a store and built a couple of cottages, making a nucleus for a large auto camp."

[F. B. Osborne came to the valley from Pomona around 1928. His homestead was where Norris Bakko later built his Chevron Station, across from La Casa del Zorro. The *Ramona Sentinel* (September 19, 1930) reports that he had "the nucleus of a fine auto camp, filling station and grocery store." The Osbornes also had the only piano in the valley. His daughter, Gladys, was very active in community affairs.]

LELAH PORTER

The pump house and water tank on the Bowers Ranch in the 1930s, located along the east side of what is now DiGiorgio Road.

"Fred Lanz, proprietor of the Tubb [sic] Canyon ranch, is developing a fine gravity water supply from Tubb creek and is raising winter tomatoes for the Ramona market."

[Fred Lanz was the "Tomato King" of the Borego Valley in the 1930s. He settled in Tub (one b) Canyon in the late '20s, and began marketing his crops by 1930. He remained around the valley well into the 1940s.]

"Charles and Henry Fearney, owners of the Palm Canyon ranch, have extensive plans for the development of their property, with plans to secure water by gravity from [Borrego] Palm [Canyon] creek.... "

[The Fearneys' ranch was near the mouth of Borrego Palm Canyon, about where the state park campground is today. The brothers acquired the property in the late 1920s, but did not spend

The Harry Oliver adobe under construction, 1930.

much time in the valley. In 1930, Charles was living in Altadena and Henry was in Rhode Island. Charles eventually began to spend more time in the valley, and in 1939 was elected justice of the peace. They grew a variety of vegetables on their ranch; in 1933 they were shipping cucumbers.]

"Emil Christiansen is digging a well at present and plans to raise winter tomatoes upon his property when this well is completed.

"Frank Scheck has completed a small well upon his property and is raising a small planting of tomatoes.

"Fay Childers has built a fine new home upon the Thompson ranch and is planning to drill a well and engage in the raising of poultry for outside markets.

"John Windolph has built a new house upon his ranch and developed a small well.... "

[Emil Christiansen, one of the older settlers in Borego, purchased his ranch in 1929 and lived in the valley for most of the 1930s. He eventually got into turkey raising. Frank Scheck homesteaded around 1929 up on the alluvial fan where Rams Hill is now located. He moved to the valley in 1930 and died in 1936. Fay

Childers also came to the valley in 1930, but left around 1932. Childers was one of several female homesteaders in the area. Among the others were Nora Carpenter and her mother, Mary Merritt; Helen Jones; and back in the 'teens, Doc Beaty's sister, Sarah. John Windolph was one of several earlier Borego homesteaders who came back after the valley began to be settled in the 1920s. He had originally homesteaded around 1915, and came back and built a new home in 1930. He sold all of his property to Roy Ensign in 1931, except ten acres around his home.]

"The Julian-Kane Springs highway, now an actuality, has stimulated the endeavors of the people of Borego and is bringing inquiries from hundreds of new people desirous of locating in Borego, according to Lloyd E. Kelsey, corresponding secretary of the Borego chamber of commerce.

"The citizens of the valley are also contemplating joining with the city of San Diego in assisting in the payments of the cost of a pipe line from the canals of the Imperial Irrigation district and securing an ample water supply to irrigate several thousand acres of the valley's fertile lands. This improvement will add materially to the assessable wealth of the county and insure prosperity for this area....

"The crop range for Borego valley is so varied in its character that settlement and development will be quite rapid as soon as the proper transportation facilities are provided with the completion of the Julian-Kane Springs highway project.

"The valley possesses a live chamber of commerce, headed by Milo C. Porter as president, with Medford Courtney and Mrs. Lloyd McGinnis as vice presidents, Mrs. Medford B. Courtney, treasurer, and Miss Drilla DuVall, secretary. It has a fine elementary school for the grammar grades with an excellent high school nearby at Julian. Veterans of the valley are also planning on organizing an American Legion post. A very fine community spirit exists here and a hearty welcome is extended to prospective settlers."

DESERT ROADS

The key to all these projects and plans was the new roads that were slowly being built across the desert. The most important was the Julian-Kane Springs Road (now State Highway 78). Some work had been done on the route as early as 1913, and plans for an automobile road were being discussed as early as 1917. The construction of the "old red bridge" in Sentenac Canyon in 1922 began to make the route a reality. In 1925 a road was opened down past The Narrows and on into Imperial County, south of today's modern highway. It left a lot to be desired. "When you get down from The Narrows out toward Imperial Valley," Lelah Porter recalls, "you run into clay, you're not on sand at all, it's just old adobe clay, and oh, the chuckholes were worse than sand! It was just one chuckhole after the other. It was a terrible road."[45]

In 1928 Borego's homesteaders began to lobby both San Diego and Imperial Counties to improve the road. The plan became a political football according to Porter: "In 1928 Felix Landis was running for [County] Supervisor...and a fellow by the name of [Leroy]

LELAH PORTER

The original bridge in Sentenac Canyon, built in 1922. The old footings are still visible across the creek from the modern bridge.

Aul ran against him. And he ran saying that if he got in he would macadamize the roads.... Well, of course for the people in Borego that was a big thing, because if you wanted to go to Brawley it was about a four- or five-hour drive the way it was. So there were sixty-two voters in our precinct, and Aul got sixty-one votes. My husband and I campaigned hard for Mr. Aul, and he knew it. We had a meeting down there, everybody came, and the women all brought food, and Mr. Aul came down and talked to us. So in the election, Landis had won until the Borego votes got in, and with sixty-one votes coming in for Aul he was elected. So he sent me a box of candy."[46]

BORREGO SUN

Charles Bemis out rolling rocks while driving into the valley, circa 1920.

In September, 1929, the county established its first prison "Honor Farm" road camp near Yaqui Well. The site is now an Anza-Borrego Desert State Park campground, and the tamarisk trees planted for the road camp gave it its modern name, Tamarisk Grove.

SAN DIEGO HISTORICAL SOCIETY RESEARCH ARCHIVES

The new Borego Valley prison camp at what is now Tamarisk Grove, 1929.

The *Ramona Sentinel* described the new camp shortly after its opening, hailing it as "a model of housing and scientific arrangement for the purpose for which it is designed.

"The prisoner's camp embraces a little over an acre in area and is inclosed by an eight foot barbed wire fence. Over the entrance the word 'Stop' is posted in large letters....

"The...most interesting [building] is the substantial building that is the cage and prisoners' dormitory, consisting of corrugated iron roofing and walls re-enforced with steel throughout, and a cement floor. Within this building are a line of triple bunks made of steel built over each other where the prisoners sleep. Four pairs of blankets are issued to each worker and each is required to make his bed and assist in keeping the quarters sanitary.... There is a radio to entertain the prisoners in the evening.... "[47]

Beginning with nothing but hand tools, the prisoners hacked out a roadbed along the south side of San Felipe Creek. By the summer of 1931, sixty men were on the job. Later, contractors with heavy equipment were brought in, and the road was extended out across the desert. It was not until 1932 that the job was finished. A year later, the state took control of the road and declared it a state highway.

Beginning with nothing but hand tools, the prisoners hacked out a roadbed along the south side of San Felipe Creek. By the summer of 1931, sixty men were on the job. It was not until 1932 that the job was finished.

The opening of the original Julian-Kane Springs Road in 1925 probably spurred the development of the Little Borego townsite, which was laid out in 1926. Several buildings were built on the townsite, including a store, a school and the fourteen-room Miracle Hotel.[48] All around the townsite were five- and ten-acre "farms," offered at low down and easy payments. But the final route of the new highway by-passed the townsite by several miles, and the coming of the Depression marked the end of the project. Early in 1932 a gas station opened near the highway construction camp. This was the beginning of modern Ocotillo Wells. By 1937 Ed Benson was running a service station along the new highway. He sold out at the end of 1944, but his name survives in nearby Benson Dry Lake.

Before Highway 78 was complete, the Borego homesteaders had built another road for themselves out across the Borrego Badlands to join State Highway 99 (now Highway 86) near a little gas station called Truckhaven. As usual, Doc Beaty was the one who pushed the hardest to get the project started, and once the job began, he worked harder on it than anyone else. According to Beaty's wife, Frances, in 1929, "Mr. Beaty and Lloyd Kelsey went over the tax books and land office records [to] get the names of owners in the valley, then they went to each one and asked for donations in either work or money, and everyone responded wonderfully. They went to the merchants of various towns and they all donated willingly. The main object was to get a road out to a town like Coachella or Indio, as San Diego County had refused to help us with roads."[49]

SAN DIEGO HISTORICAL SOCIETY PHOTOGRAPHIC COLLECTION

A tractor accident during the construction of the Truckhaven Trail, 1930.

Most of the residents of the valley had a hand in the construction of what they called the "Borego Road." As the work carried them further and further out of the valley, the women followed their husbands into the Badlands to cook for the construction camp. Lelah Porter, pregnant with her second child, was spared cooking in the road camp, but still recalls:

"This end of it was just a matter of grading, and they did a lot of it with fresnos. Doc had a couple of teams and they did a lot of it by hand. But when they got over to the Imperial County side they ran into those deep washes. Now they bridge those. Milo worked on it when they were building there, and they had to go with the fresnos down the side of those washes. You don't go straight down, you angle down, then they'd turn and angle up the other side. There were three of them. I think it took as much time to build the road through those three canyons as it did to build the rest of the road, if I remember right."[50] Even when it was completed in 1930, "It was a slow road," Porter concedes. "I don't suppose you could drive over twenty miles an hour over it, if you could drive that fast."[51]

According to a 1930 accounting, the entire project cost about $750, with a remaining deficit of $26.60.[52] On June 22, 1930, a barbecue was held at Doc Beaty's Coyote Canyon ranch to celebrate the completion of the road. Borego homesteader and poet laureate Nora Carpenter marked the occasion with one of her many poems, which she read to the crowd of more than one hundred:

Welcome, friends, to our Borego
We're not far from San Diego
But it's quite a little journey to L.A.
And the road was so durned pore
It made Boregoans good and sore
So they up and built this shorter better way....

So the men all got together
Didn't stop for any weather
For they worked in rain and snow and in the blazing sun
Grubbed the cactus, scraped the sands
Got big blisters on their hands
Worked like demons 'till they got this road all done.

And when it was hot as hades
To the road camp came the ladies,
Two by two, and ran the cook stove with a snap
Fed the men on such good chow
They could do their work - and how
Thus they helped to put Borego on the map.

Everyone deserves great praise
All have helped, in various ways
Our "Doc" Beaty was the one to start the load
Then the rest at his appeals
Put their shoulders to the wheels
And today we all may ride along this road.

"All roads lead to Rome" 'twas said,
Tho' this saying's long been dead
We can use it here in county San Diego
If we all with one accord
Pull just like a brand new Ford
Until 'tis said all roads lead to Borego.[53]

But the glory days of the Truckhaven Trail were brief. With the completion of Highway 78 in 1932, the unpaved and wash-out-prone Truckhaven route fell into disuse.

Another road that was discussed for many years was the Yaqui Pass Road, though construction did not begin until 1933. The county began the project, but soon halted until funding from the State Emergency Relief Administration (SERA) became available in 1934. A number of local homesteaders, including Doc Beaty, Hugh Butz and Al Mathes did most of the work, which crept along through the winter of 1934-35. The Yaqui Pass Road later became the first paved road into the valley.

These new roads did much to provide better access to Borego, but despite repeated pleas to the county Board of Supervisors, when it came to roads in the valley itself, Judge Kelsey pointed out, "It looks as though the residents of the valley must work out their own salvation."[54]

Lelah Porter recalls that when she arrived in 1927, "there were no roads in the valley." An old hogback road climbed out of The Narrows and reached the valley near what is now La Casa del Zorro. From there, Porter says, "you angled up to the Ensign Ranch...and then you just angled on up to Coyote Canyon. It wasn't on section lines at all. So if you wanted a road you took off across the desert, and if you could make it without getting stuck, well the next guy would follow your tracks and that was a road!"[55]

The first properly surveyed and built road in the valley was what is now Palm Canyon Drive, which followed the township line between Townships 10 and 11. O. H. Ensign paid for the survey and may well have paid for the road, too. It was completed in January, 1930. The Ensigns, Dana Burks, Harry Oliver and other local ranchers continued to build more and better roads through the valley as the '30s wore on.[56]

THE DANA BURKS RANCH

During the construction of Highway 78, the Borrego Valley caught the eye of Dana Burks, a Los Angeles and Palm Springs real estate developer. In 1932 he and a group of investors acquired the rights to 13,500 acres of railroad lands in and around the valley, much of it raw, desert land. Burks hoped to entice both agriculture and resort living to the valley. Agriculturally, he was relying on Borego's desert climate, which would allow grapes, tomatoes and other crops to be harvested early and reach the markets ahead of other growers' crops. "We are not interested in growing anything that will not beat the market," Burks told the *San Diego Union*. "We feel that here we can ripen our products at any time we desire, selecting our own market and assuring it."[57]

(In an era in which fruits and vegetables are flown into the United States from across the globe, the idea of "beating the market" may be foreign to some younger readers. Before the 1960s, when most fruits and vegetables were still available only when they were in season, whoever got their produce to the market first got the best prices for it. The warmer climate thus gave desert farmers a jump on their coastal competitors. The drive to "beat the market" would remain a key factor in the agricultural history of the Borrego Valley for decades to come.)

Burks also hoped the valley would become a center of resort living. His vision sounds like some of the later publicity for Borrego Springs: "Burks [en]visions the valley as a great winter playground, dotted with productive desert estates and encircled by the wild, mountainous desolation of the Borego desert [state] park. An authentic Spanish flavor of architecture and development will match the landscape, according to his plan, and the settlers will be specialists in agriculture and in living the fullness of desert life."[58]

But the bottom of the Depression was no time to be launching a new, isolated desert development, and Burks soon became discouraged. In 1937 he sold his own Spanish-style adobe (built in 1933) to Noel Crickmer (1902-1988). Crickmer had been the manager of the Del Mar Hotel on the San Diego coast. In later years he liked to claim that there were only twenty-five people living in the valley when he arrived. "The valley wasn't dead, it was lifeless."[59] This was an exaggeration, but certainly Borego in the late 1930s was a pretty

BORREGO SUN

Dana Burks' adobe ranch house, built in 1933. Portions of it survive as the entrance to La Casa del Zorro.

Desert Lodge — ancestor of La Casa del Zorro

quiet place. Still, in 1939, Crickmer and his wife, Ruth, decided to open Borego's first hotel, the Desert Lodge—the ancestor of today's La Casa del Zorro. In 1940 they added four more guest rooms. Electricity came from a generator, and milk came from the Crickmers' cow. "[T]he most we could offer guests were good beds, an ample supply of food and a friendly desert atmosphere," Crickmer later recalled. "We planned picnics and excursions in order that our guests could imbibe desert pleasures to the fullest."[60]

BORREGO SUN

Yaqui Pass Road sweeps downhill past the new sign for the Desert Lodge, circa 1940.

Adventurous tourists from San Diego began to discover the valley. Then came World War II, and the Desert Lodge was crowded with military officers and their families. The Crickmers sold out to the Burnand family in 1947. Portions of Dana Burks' original adobe still stand today as part of the lobby of La Casa del Zorro.

> "
> **[T]he most we could offer guests were good beds, an ample supply of food and a friendly desert atmosphere."**
>
> ***Noel Crickmer***

Borego's other big booster was Harry Woods (1874-1964), a real estate agent who first visited the valley in 1925. "If it hadn't been for him I don't think the valley would have progressed at all," says Lelah Porter.[61] "Silk Hat Harry," as Lloyd Kelsey jokingly dubbed him, encouraged a number of new homesteaders and developers to come into the valley, including Dana Burks, A. A. Burnand, G. M. Jones and the Fearneys. His son, Fred Woods, was later a Borrego Springs real estate agent for many years.

BOREGO STATE PARK

Just as the Borrego Valley was beginning to fill up with homesteads in the late 1920s, efforts began to preserve some of the surrounding desert for future generations. In 1927, C. C. Abbott of the San Diego Natural History Museum toured the area with Doc Beaty as his guide. Abbott was impressed with what he saw, especially in Borrego Palm Canyon, and the drive began to establish California's first desert state park.

Abbott and Guy Fleming, also of the Natural History Museum, became the most vocal supporters of the creation of the new state park. Lloyd Kelsey, Harry Woods, Henry Fearney and others soon joined them in talking up the plan. Kelsey described the beauties of Borrego Palm Canyon for readers of the *San Diego Union*:

"Snugly tucked away in a rugged rocky fastness of the San Ysidro mountains lies Palm canyon, which despite its virtual isolation has been an irresistible lure to hundreds of San Diegans seeking new fields to explore.

LELAH PORTER

By the early 1930s, a few hardy tourists were already coming down to the valley to view the annual wildflower bloom.

"So thought...the writer...as [I] viewed with amazed eyes these tawny palm trees, clustered among giant monoliths, battling for existence during centuries, against storms of wind and water.

"Trickling its way amid these marvelous specimens of a bygone age is a mountain stream, clear and icy, to lose itself in the valley sands below. The canyon, inviting further exploration, we went up and up, more palms greeting us at every turn. A thousand there must be there....

"Winding our way among the giant boulders, oftimes [sic] clambering over seemingly impossible places and parting drooping palm fronds we finally arrived at a wonderful pool of clear, cold water nearly 100 feet long and half that wide and quite deep, completely surrounded by stately palm trees, making an ideal setting of tropic splendor for some eastern potentate's palace garden....

"These trees, in their almost perfect natural setting, should be preserved for all posterity and the people of San Diego county should take some steps to insure their permanent care by their inclusion in some park site."[62]

> **"These trees, in their almost perfect natural setting, should be preserved for all posterity and the people of San Diego county should take some steps to insure their permanent care by their inclusion in some park site."**
>
> ***Lloyd Kelsey***

It was probably also Kelsey who reported in the *Ramona Sentinel* on July 6, 1928, "The proposed new park in Palm canyon has been bringing in a number of visitors the past week. Palm canyon would make an ideal winter park, with the beautiful wild flowers we have here in the winter, and no fogs—nothing but the balmy old sunshine."

The tourists continued to come, and in 1928 San Diego County voters helped pass California's first state park bond act. In 1932 the State of California accepted the first parcel of what would become the park, and in 1933 the Borego Palms Desert State Park, as it was originally known, was created after the acquisition of 185,000 acres of federal land surrounding the valley. Fleming became the Southern

District Superintendent for the California State Parks, serving from 1933 to 1948. His son, John Fleming, along with Paul McEwen, became the first two "custodians" of the new desert park. In 1935 and '36 a Civilian Conservation Corps camp was established on the Fearney ranch, and the "C.C.C. boys" were put to work developing the park's first campground. The stone shade ramadas they built still stand in Borrego Palm Canyon Campground.

The original parklands were all located north of Highway 78, but in 1936 another 365,000 acres of federal land, stretching south to the Vallecito and Carrizo valleys, was made available. The Borrego name no longer seemed sufficient for the enlarged park, so the park was renamed the Anza Desert State Park in 1938.[63]

Not everyone in Borego, or in San Diego County, was originally in favor of the park, and the proposed Vallecito/Carrizo expansion was hotly contested. The usual argument was that it was taking valuable agricultural land off the county tax rolls. Others pointed out that if it was so valuable, why were there only three families living in the area—the Campbells, the Crawfords and Marshal South and his family living their "primitive" life on top of Ghost Mountain? After a series of battles and delay tactics, the southern acreage was finally transferred to the state park in 1941.

After a series of seasonal custodians, in 1936 Jack Calvert was assigned to the park as its first permanent ranger. He spent his winters in Borrego and his summers at Lake Tahoe, while the Borego State Park was officially "closed." Calvert did much to win over those residents of Borego who were still skeptical about the growing park. From 1944 to 1946 Calvert was stationed at the old mission at La Purisima State Historic Park, and John Fleming filled in for the winters while he was gone. But in the fall of 1946 Calvert returned to Borrego and remained until his retirement in 1952.[64]

In 1938, the Borego Chamber of Commerce took it upon itself to dedicate the new state park. Milo Porter's uncle, John C. Porter, a former mayor of Los Angeles, was then serving on the State Park Commission, so he was invited as the speaker for the day. "We decided we were going to dedicate the state park," Lelah Porter

The Borego Valley Chamber of Commerce's unofficial "dedication" of the Anza Desert State Park during the Ocotillo Days celebration, April, 1938. The make-shift stage was used by the school children who presented part of the program that day.

recalls, "...and the teacher wrote a little play, and the kids were in the play, and we fixed our truck up as a stage. And Milo's uncle and aunt came down and were there, and Jack Calvert, the first park ranger, he was there. And so we dedicated the park. All it was then was Palm Canyon.... It didn't mean a thing, because it was just our local chamber of commerce that did it, but the kids put on the play and we had a nice little program."[65]

The park did help to focus a little more attention on the Borrego Valley in the 1930s, and a few hardy tourists began coming down, especially during wildflower season each spring. In April of 1934 the Borego Chamber of Commerce began hosting "Ocotillo Days" for the tourists during wildflower time. The annual celebration continued throughout the remainder of the decade. In 1938 an estimated fifteen hundred to two thousand cars were in the valley for the celebration.

THE WAR YEARS

As the Depression of the 1930s wore on, the little homesteader community of Borego continued to decline. Some of the ranchers with outside capital, such as the Ensigns, did all right. Other homesteaders hung on, doing what they could to get by.[66] Many others left the valley. Between 1931 and 1939 the Borego Precinct lost two-thirds of its registered voters, more than one hundred people.[67] With the coming of World War II, the pioneer homesteader days in Borego came to an end.

In 1941, the first stirrings of World War II began to reach the desert. That spring the Navy made its first request to the State Park Commission to use park lands for aerial training exercises. By 1945, nearly all of Anza Desert State Park was under military control. Author F. L. Orrell, who made a special study of the war years in the park, notes, "...they asked for the land and it was handed to them.... It was as easy for the military to gain access to tens of thousands of acres as to a section."[68] Benson and Clark dry lakes were designated as emergency landing fields, and bombing ranges were also established at both places. The targets and observation positions are still visible on Clark Dry Lake. Practice bombing runs were also made in

BORREGO SUN

"Camp Ensign," the temporary Marine training outpost established on the Ensign Ranch in 1943.

and around what is now known as Military Wash, north of Borrego Mountain.

The Army established the Borego Maneuver Area early in 1942. Anti-aircraft units from Camp Callan at Torrey Pines practiced firing at radio-controlled drone aircraft out across the Borrego Badlands. The Army also sponsored rocket tests in the Military Wash area. With North Africa selected as the allies' first target, desert training was deemed essential, though one field artillery battalion sent down for desert training in the early months of the war was then shipped out to Alaska.

BORREGO SUN

Military vehicles were a regular sight around DuVall's store during World War II.

Some of the Army units stayed on the Ensign Ranch, and in 1943 the Marines took over the northeast corner of the ranch, near the Borego School. They built a more elaborate base camp that was generally, though apparently unofficially, known as Camp Ensign. Where Army trainees had slept in poncho-covered foxholes, the Marines erected sleeping quarters and mess tents. During 1943 and 1944, Marines from Camp Pendleton and Camp Elliott would spend about a week at a time on the desert, working on nighttime driving skills across the Badlands.[69]

One fringe benefit of all this military activity in the valley was the paving of the Yaqui Pass Road in 1942. From the Desert Lodge, the paving continued up along what is now Rango Way, and out Borrego Valley Road to Palm Canyon Drive. From there, the paving continued east and then around the curve north to Peg Leg.

The arrival of the valley's first paved road marks the symbolic end of the little homesteader community of Borego. The population seems to have bottomed out around 1943, then slowly began to grow again. By the end of the war, plans were already in motion that would change life in the Borrego Valley forever.

NOTES

1. Frances Beaty, who came to the valley in 1913, later wrote that the water from Borrego Spring was "warm and brackish, but across the creek there was a well that one of the McCain brothers had dug for domestic purposes. The water stood within a foot of the surface of the ground. It was sweet and even on the hottest day the water was cold." (*Borrego Sun*, March, 1955)
2. Some local tracts were filed on under the Desert Land Act, first enacted in 1877, which allowed entries of up to 320 acres. There was no residency requirement, but claimants had to develop a water supply and make other improvements totaling three dollars an acre.
3. Personal interview, November 19, 1986 (for the Anza-Borrego Desert Natural History Association). Frances Beaty later said it took them five days to make the trip from Azusa, and when they arrived there were just five families living in the valley (notes from a talk, 1953. Copy courtesy Virginia DeMarais).
4. Personal interview, November 19, 1986.
5. Personal interview, November 19, 1986.
6. Personal interview, November 19, 1986. See also my articles on Beaty in the *Borrego Sun*, June 16, 30, 1994.
7. Handwritten notes, circa 1953, in the DeMarais Collection. Charles Bemis (1850-1925) was one of the pioneer settlers of Covina. He had a 320-acre Desert Land Act claim in the southeast part of the valley.
8. Virginia DeMarais dated this first school "around 1915" (*Borrego Sun*, October 22, 1992). Frances Beaty remembered the date as 1917 (notes courtesy Virginia DeMarais).
9. *Ramona Sentinel*, June 8, 1928. The *Sentinel's* "Borego Valley News" column had begun just one week before, made possible by the regular mail service in and out of the valley, which had begun that spring. Lloyd Kelsey was probably Borego's original correspondent, and the column carried his by-line from 1931 until his death in August, 1932. Lloyd's father, Judge J. A. Kelsey, took over in 1933, and kept writing until his death in January, 1937. After that, sadly, the Borego column in the *Sentinel* comes to an end.
10. Personal interview, May 3, 1994.
11. Personal interview, July 28, 1995.
12. *Ramona Sentinel*, January 18, 1929.
13. *Ramona Sentinel*, August 16, 1929. A miner's "inch" of water is equivalent to nine flowing gallons per minute.
14. *Ramona Sentinel*, December 6, 1929.
15. *Ramona Sentinel*, December 20, 1929.

16. *Ramona Sentinel*, July 12, 1929. As late as 1954, the Ensigns still had one hundred acres in alfalfa, and were cutting every twenty-one days during the six most productive months of the year.
17. Philip Curti, *The Borrego Valley: The Birth of a Desert Community* (unpublished Master's Thesis, University of California, Los Angeles), 1955.
18. Curti, *The Borrego Valley*, 1955.
19. *Ramona Sentinel*, September 20, 1929.
20. Personal interview, November 19, 1986. On January 27, 1933, the *Ramona Sentinel* reported: "A. A. Beaty reports that all the pecan trees planted by him last spring which did not get the required growth owing to the lateness of the planting, will soon be removed..."
21. *Borrego Sun*, November 4, 1993. Alfred Armstrong McCandless was a Riverside County Supervisor from 1970-82 and a United States Congressman from 1982 until his retirement in 1994. He spent a great deal of time on his grandfather's homestead, and even attended the Borrego Valley School in the early 1930s.
22. *Ramona Sentinel*, November 10, 1933.
23. *Ramona Sentinel*, March 3, 1933.
24. Kanemaru's name is spelled various ways in the newspapers of the time. In the 1935 *San Diego County Directory* it is spelled Kanemura.
25. Personal interview, July 27, 1983.
26. *Ramona Sentinel*, July 28, 1933.
27. Wynn had been a jeweler in Azusa before coming to the valley around 1914. Doc Beaty had also come from Azusa, which may explain why Wynn first came to Borego.
28. *Ramona Sentinel*, January 17, 1930. The storm dropped nearly four inches of snow in the center of Borrego Valley.
29. Personal interview, March 1, 1999.
30. Personal interview, July 29, 1994. Judge Kelsey noted in the *Ramona Sentinel* (January 24, 1935), "We are sorry to note the untimely death of our pioneer merchant and postmaster, and Valley mail carrier, Eslie Wynn, which occurred suddenly last Saturday evening from a heart attack."
31. Speaking at the Borego Founders Day, October 14, 1995.
32. Personal conversation, February 4, 1997.
33. *Borrego Sun*, May, 1950. "There were 22 children the first year," Margaret Boch recalls, "and Miss Woolsey taught us all."
34. *Ramona Sentinel*, December 21, 1928.
35. *Ramona Sentinel*, December 15, 1933.
36. *Ramona Sentinel*, February 9, 1934.

37. Personal interview, July 29, 1994. Virginia DeMarais told a similar story in the *Borrego Sun* (October 22, 1992): "The district asked Dana Burks for two acres to put the school on, but that donation eventually ended up at 20 acres with the suggestion that part of the land could be used for a park and community center and also some acreage for a local cemetery."
38. School notes, dated July 25, 1964 (copy courtesy Lelah Porter).
39. Personal interview, May 3, 1994.
40. *San Diego Union*, February 5, 1931.
41. Prior to the formation of the Borego Township, in 1928, Tom Miller had been hired by the county as Borego's first deputy sheriff. When he left the valley in the spring of 1930, John Freeman got the job, serving until the township was created.
42. *Ramona Sentinel*, December 20, 1929.
43. Copy in the DeMarais Collection (Ensign file). A second, revised version of the brochure was issued in 1933.
44. Personal interview, July 29, 1994. Sleepy Hollow is still on some maps, in the hilly country east of the Borrego Sink. The Borrego Air Ranch is there today.
45. Personal interview, July 28, 1995.
46. Personal interview, July 29, 1994. At the time, the *Union* called the race for the Third District seat, "The hottest battle of the election..." (November 7, 1928). Aul finally won, 2,391 to 2,291. Aul served only one term as a supervisor, losing his bid for reelection in 1932.
47. *Ramona Sentinel*, November 15, 1929. A later (August 14, 1931) feature notes that if any of the prisoners escaped, a fifty-dollar reward would be paid for their capture, collected out of the remaining prisoners' wages. The prisoners were receiving thirty-five cents a day. The Borego Valley Prison Camp was closed in 1933 and converted into a county road station.
48. Lelah Porter maintains the developers were forced to build the hotel because they had promised one in all their early advertising. The hotel seems to have disappeared sometime in the '40s, but the foundation is still visible.
49. Frances Beaty, letter to Horace Parker, December 11, 1957, Horace Parker Papers, Sherman Library & Gardens, Corona del Mar, California.
50. Personal interview, July 28, 1995.
51. Personal interview, July 28, 1995.
52. "Financial Statement of Borego Road" (copy courtesy Fleta Beaty McCandless). Some of the outside donors included businesses in Brawley, Westmorland, Indio, Coachella, Julian and the Truckhaven Service Station itself. The Indio Chamber of Commerce gave fifty-four dollars. The Hollywood crowd (Oliver et al.) put up about seventy-five dollars. Doc Beaty gave almost $140 besides all the work he did.

53. Typescript copy courtesy Fleta Beaty McCandless. Carpenter had donated five dollars towards the project and may have worked in the road camp as well.
54. *Ramona Sentinel*, February 14, 1935.
55. Personal interview, May 3, 1994.
56. The upper end of what is now Borrego Valley Road was built in 1932, along with Peg Leg Road from Palm Canyon Drive up towards Clark Dry Lake. Harry Oliver began applying names to the valley roads in 1929. In sorting out the scattered early references, Palm Canyon Drive seems to have begun life as Cahuilla Road. Borrego Valley Road was named Dickerson Boulevard when it was built, in honor of John Dickerson, a 1910-era Borego homesteader. Later it was known as Schoolhouse Road. Peg Leg Road was originally known as Hoboyak Road, after a legendary Cupeño Indian leader from the Warner Springs area. DiGiorgio Road seems to have been known as Anza Road into the 1950s. Crowley Road is also mentioned in the early 1930s, named for George Crowley, then the superintendent of the Dana Burks ranch. This may have been today's Rango Way.
57. *San Diego Union*, March 19, 1933. Burks and his associates had already planted thirty acres of grape vines, and were considering tomatoes, squash, peas, cucumbers, and sweet potatoes.
58. *San Diego Union*, March 19, 1933. Burks was still boosting Borego in 1937, talking of resort hotels and breeding farms for polo ponies (*Ramona Sentinel*, December 2, 1937). He remained active in valley affairs through the rest of the decade, and died sometime in the 1940s.
59. *Borrego Sun*, July 31, 1971.
60. *Borrego Sun*, August 14, 1971.
61. Personal interview, July 29, 1994.
62. *San Diego Union*, December 28, 1930.
63. From 1953 to 1957 the park was split in two. The northern portion was known as the Borrego State Park, while the southern end (with its headquarters at the old county road camp site at Tamarisk Grove) retained the old Anza Desert State Park name. When the two halves were reassembled in 1957, the park was renamed the Anza-Borrego Desert State Park. For the history of the creation of the park, see Diana Lindsay's 1973 book, *Our Historic Desert. The Story of the Anza-Borrego Desert* (San Diego: Copley Books). See also her article, "The Creation of the Anza Borrego Desert State Park," in the *Journal of San Diego History*, Fall, 1973.

64. Calvert, a World War I veteran, had previously worked for the United States Forest Service before joining the young California State Park system in the mid-1930s. A former resident of Azusa, he made his first trip to the valley in 1919, when he helped fellow Azusan Eslie Wynn dig a well. His wife, Ella (the namesake of Ella Wash out in the Borrego Badlands), later wrote, "Of all the parks where he has served, he really loves Anza Desert best." (*News and Views* [State of California Department of Natural Resources Division of Beaches and Parks newsletter], April, 1949).

65. Personal interviews, July 29, 1994, and July 28, 1995. According to Diana Lindsay, the state finally officially dedicated the park in December, 1941.

66. Even before the Depression, getting by for the homesteaders meant sometimes hunting out of season for deer and even the occasional bighorn sheep. Fleta Beaty McCandless admitted to that particular skeleton in most of the old families' closets: "In those days, boy, it was something. I'll tell you why; you know, when you live on just beans and rabbits or whatever kind of meat you could get, why, dad would get so hungry for some fresh meat that he'd take off and pretty near always come back with something. And he knew he was breaking the law, but fortunately for him he never got caught." (Personal interview, November 19, 1986). Old time cattleman Bud Clark told me the local game warden was always out to catch Beaty, but never did. Al McCandless recalls that his family more often ate rattlesnake and rabbits—"My grandmother probably knew 40 ways to cook a rabbit, and I ate rabbit prepared each one of the 40 ways as a child. I don't eat rabbit anymore." (*Borrego Sun*, November 4, 1993).

67. According to the *San Diego Union* (February 5, 1931; January 24, 1939), the number of registered voters in the Borego Township dropped from 148 in 1931 to just forty-five in 1939. The Borego listings in the yearly San Diego County directories show a similar story. The local listings more than double between 1930 and 1931—from forty-eight to one hundred—then drop each year until they bottom out in 1935 at just forty-five. Then the numbers start to slowly climb again, reaching seventy-seven by 1938—the last year there is a separate listing for Borego. Both voter registration and directory listings are for the larger Borego Township (which included the Ocotillo Wells area), but most of the population was always in the valley. In 1931 the *San Diego Union* estimated the population of the township at three hundred.

68. F. L. Orrell, *Recent Military Operations in the Anza-Borrego Desert State Park* (unpublished report, prepared with a James Brainerd Grant from the Anza-Borrego Desert Natural History Association, 1991). Most of the material in this section comes from Orrell's report.

69. Despite repeated assertions, there is no evidence that General Patton ever directed training on the Borrego Desert. His operations were all on the Mojave Desert.

PART II

BORREGO SPRINGS
Your Place in the Sun

THE BIRTH OF BORREGO SPRINGS

The dream of an attractive desert community in the Borrego Valley had been around since the days of Dana Burks, but it took A. A. Burnand to make that dream a reality. "You have to take your hat off to him," longtime Borrego realtor Fred Woods later said. "He...gambled when no one else would gamble. He stuck it out...I can't give enough credit to him. Burnand had the fortitude to stick with it."[1]

> **"He [A. A. Burnand]... gambled when no one else would gamble. He stuck it out...I can't give enough credit to him. Burnand had the fortitude to stick with it."**
>
> ***Fred Woods***

Alphonse A. Burnand, Jr., had been born in Leadville, Colorado, in 1896, where his Swiss-born father worked as a mining assayer. Before he was ten years old, Burnand's family moved to Santa Monica, California. After considering a career in engineering, Burnand ended up studying agriculture at the University of California at Davis. After graduation, he liked to recall, "I started out in a Model T Ford with a collie pup and ended up in Delano. Before I knew it, I was behind a plow."[2]

Table grapes were the principal crop in the area, and Burnand soon acquired his own vineyard two miles north of Delano. Burnand not only grew grapes, he marketed his crop to wholesale buyers across the country. After a few years, he also began to handle the marketing for other small growers in the area.

The big grape growers in the Central Valley were the DiGiorgio family. "At that time the DiGiorgios were the largest grape growers in the world," says Burnand's son, A. A. "Al" Burnand III. "They had something like twenty thousand acres, and he just became friends with them, and they liked each other, and it developed from there."[3]

In the mid-1920s Burnand hired a Japanese foreman to run his Delano vineyards, moved to Los Angeles and expanded his shipping and marketing business to Nogales, Arizona, where he handled tomatoes raised by growers in Sonora, Mexico.

A. A. Burnand first visited the Borrego Valley around 1933, at the suggestion of one of his employees, Al Way, who had been out looking for an "early" growing area for Burnand's grapes. "Dad always said he was one of the smartest viticulturists that he knew," says Al Burnand. He visited Roy Brininger's ranch, and found grapes ripening a full month ahead of his Central Valley vineyards. So in 1936, A. A. Burnand bought an interest in Doc Beaty's old Coyote Canyon ranch.

Wes Buerkle, another Burnand associate, recalled in 1956: "[T]wenty years ago, brother Bill and I, in partnership with Alphonse Burnand, Jr., were crazy enough to try farming in Borrego Valley. At that time, there was little more than the Ensign Date Ranch, and, of course, Ed DuVall, our deputy sheriff, and the Brininger Ranch.

"The residence of the late Mr. Brininger was an oasis if I ever saw one. This, together with the glib tongue of Harry Woods, convinced us to try to produce grapes here. We purchased the De Anza Ranch at the head of the valley and proceeded to farm grapes. By mid-April the grapes looked wonderful. The next day the wind came up and the grapes went down.

"With plenty of water from the stream in Coyote Creek, we soon had eighty percent of them growing again. But, in May, the wind came up again and forgot to stop and the grape vines forgot to grow; so Brother Bill and I left the valley and returned to our farming business in Bakersfield to recoup our finances and increase our supply of brains, but we came back.

"Burnand's enthusiasm was not dampened and he hired a man to take over where we left off. Alas and alack, without windbreaks the young vines could not get started. By then, however, Burnand had spent enough time in the valley to appreciate its wonderful weather and to realize its potentialities as a resort."[4]

Burnand's first vineyard on the De Anza Ranch was washed out by a flood during World War II, before it had a chance to become commercially viable. But Burnand could see that he had found the early growing area he was looking for. He built a house on the ridge above Doc's old tent house, and with Al Way as foreman, grew early tomatoes on the ranch. He also began buying up other desert property in and around the Borrego Valley. Some of it was railroad land, some was being sold for taxes, and other parcels came from homesteaders selling out.

Sometime around 1943 Burnand began to dream of creating a desert community in the Borrego Valley. The limitations of wartime held back any actual development work for several years, however. Early in 1945 Burnand announced his plans to the press. The *San Diego Union* reported that Burnand was "ambitious to create a San Diego county rival of Palm Springs" with a resort hotel, a country club and golf course (the clubhouse plans were already drawn), and even its own airport.

"There will be two complementary phases of the desert program...," the *Union* explained. "One will be devoted to specialized farms and homesites, the other to recreation. Sale of the farms, it was claimed, will be restricted to agriculturalists of sufficient means and practical experience to cultivate crops that are adaptable to a desert climate.

"Homesites will be limited to 9 acres with restrictions which require appropriate and harmonious designs of residential construction."[5]

All of this was slated to begin after the end of the war, "when building materials are available." In the meantime, Burnand set about assembling the land needed for his new venture. The Anza Desert State Park (as it was then known) was dotted with private "inholdings," including old homesteads and railroad sections.[6] Burnand bought up these lands to trade with the state for land on

CATHERINE STRAND

Construction underway at Hoberg's, 1947.

the western edge of the Borrego Valley. Since the lands were traded on a value-for-value basis, instead of acre for acre, Burnand sometimes got as little as one acre of valley land for every ten acres of the often rocky and mountainous railroad lands. Through trades and purchases, Burnand eventually controlled some seventeen thousand acres in and around the valley.

Next, Burnand recruited an impressive list of partners and investors and formed two companies to supervise the project. The Borrego Springs Land & Development Company would own the tract and supervise the development, while the Borrego Springs Company would have charge of marketing and sales and see to day-to-day affairs on the townsite.

Joining Burnand and his wife, Clara, in the Borrego Springs Land & Development Company were Paul Grafe, president of Grafe Construction of Los Angeles, one of the "Six Companies" that built Boulder Dam, and Lawrence Barker, whose family founded Barker Brothers furniture stores. The Borrego Springs Company was headed by Palm Springs realtor Robert Ransom, the developer of the Palm Springs Plaza, with Fred Marlow, a Los Angeles developer and home builder who had recently served as a Federal Housing

Administration officer, and Pasadena developer and realtor Harrison Baker, who had been appointed a member of the State Highway Commission following his efforts in promoting Southern California's first freeway, the Arroyo Seco Parkway (now the Pasadena Freeway).[7]

Much of Burnand's immediate family also played a role in the development of Borrego Springs. His oldest son, A. A. Burnand III, was in Nogales much of the time, where the family's produce business was generating some of the cash that made Borrego Springs possible. His younger brother, Perry, became an active part of Borrego's farming community. After Burnand's second marriage, to Clara Kuhrts, several of his stepchildren and their spouses also played prominent roles in the early days of Borrego Springs. Charlotte Kuhrts and her husband, Herb Haughton, had Borrego Springs' first store. George "Bud" Kuhrts (1923-1995) worked closely with his stepfather on a number of local projects. He soon married Robert Ransom's niece, Beverly Hauser, and played an active role in valley affairs until his death. Their sister, Pat Kuhrts, eventually married Robert DiGiorgio, further strengthening the ties between the two families.

On November 4, 1946, the San Diego County Board of Supervisors approved the subdivision map for the first five-hundred-acre unit of the Borrego Springs tract. Work on roads and a water system was already underway, and resort facilities were planned "as soon as federal regulations banning construction of such structures are lifted."[8]

"At Borrego Springs," Robert Ransom told reporters in 1947, "we are starting from scratch and building a model community, planned for those who look beyond to tomorrow."[9] But the grand visions of Burnand and his partners always had to take a back seat to the hard practicalities of life in an isolated desert valley. First on the list was electricity. In May, 1945, the DiGiorgio Fruit Company approached San Diego Gas & Electric about extending service to the Borrego Valley so that they could begin developing their vineyards. Even though America was still at war in the Pacific, the project was approved by the War Production Board, and construction began that summer.[10]

1945 - Electricity

SDG&E did have a head start. The Imperial Irrigation District already had a power line along Highway 78 through The Narrows. SDG&E bought the existing line, built a substation at the foot of Yaqui Pass, and ran a fourteen-mile line into Borrego. Outside electricity arrived for the first time on the afternoon of October 19, 1945, and DiGiorgio switched on its first electric well pump that same day. The cost, much of it borne by DiGiorgio, was over half a million dollars. There were just eight customers in the valley to start. By 1952 there were over three hundred.

To supply water for the tract, Burnand formed the Borrego Springs Water Company in 1947. The company drilled two wells to begin with, the first in 1947, just east of Christmas Circle. A year later the company had just twenty-six customers. Later the company's service area was enlarged to include the De Anza Country Club and some of the other adjoining subdivisions.[11] In 1961 local voters approved the creation of the Borrego Springs Water District, primarily to guard the valley's groundwater supply against being siphoned off to other desert developments. The district was more or less dormant until 1979, when it was reactivated to take part in the development of Rams Hill. The Borrego Springs Water Company survived until 1996 when it finally was sold to the Borrego Water District.

The next pressing need was better access into and around the valley. In 1946, San Diego County agreed to build a new road, from Highway 78 across to the Desert Lodge. Borrego Springs Road, as it was dubbed, was built and oiled in 1947, but not paved until 1949. Within the tract, the Borrego Land and Development Company was responsible for laying out, grading, oiling, and eventually paving roads. By the fall of 1947, nearly fourteen miles of roads were complete.

Most of the roads in the tract were "curved to preserve natural beauty" of the desert. A. A. Burnand wanted to stay as far as he could from the arrow-straight, uniform "tract" look that was already beginning to sweep Southern California.

While Burnand's employees supervised much of the work on the townsite, he still kept an eye on everything. Rancher Sam Fortiner, who was developing his gladiola farm at the same time Borrego

Springs was being laid out, recalls how Burnand would roar into the valley from time to time and hunt up one of his foremen, K. O. Burt, who'd be out with a crew laying pipe, or whatever the job was for that day. "How's the payroll today?" Burnand would ask. "About the same as it was last week," Burt would say. "How many men?" "Well, I think we have twenty-eight working," Burt might reply. "All right," Burnand would announce, "bring 'em out!"

So Burt would line up the crew, and Burnand would talk to each one of them up and down the line. "Fernando," he might say, "how much money do we owe you?" "$72.50," might be the reply. And Burnand would pull out a wad of cash and count it out for each man. "Records," Fortiner laughs, "what are those? That's something you listen to music on! That's the way he operated."[12]

> **"Borrego Springs is being planned and developed as an ideal residential, recreational, desert resort community."**
>
> ***Early advertisement***

The marketing of Borrego Springs began in earnest in late 1946. While portraying the town as a resort community, Burnand and his partners also wanted to make it clear that Borrego Springs would be a peaceful place, perfect for a leisurely lifestyle. "[T]he jazz note will be missing at Borrego Springs," Robert Ransom told the papers. "We plan to develop a city which will preserve the beauty and peace of the desert."[13] "We think if people like the desert they want to have a little room about them," A. A. Burnand told another reporter. "Our town is laid out for comfort."[14]

Early advertisements stressed the natural beauty of the Borrego Valley:

"Borrego Springs is being planned and developed as an ideal residential, recreational, desert resort community.

"Nestled in the protection of the high mountains which rise abruptly on the west and north, and located on the gentle slopes of the foothill land, the property commands sweeping views of both the desert and the mountains surrounding the valley.

"Starting with a beautiful, clean, typical desert setting, it has been possible to combine the best of modern community planning with the natural beauty of the desert atmosphere, to provide the convenience of a modern residential development and at the same time to preserve the natural beauty and serenity of the desert setting."[15]

The first lots in Borrego Springs were offered for sale to the public on March 15, 1947. Prices started at one thousand dollars an acre, and, within a few months, four hundred thousand dollars' worth of sales were reported. The Borrego Springs Company built a sales office west of Christmas Circle, with a lawn and barbecue area out front. The building still stands in the rear at 648 Palm Canyon Drive.

Robert Ransom's niece, Beverly Hauser (soon to be Mrs. Bud Kuhrts), had been working for him at Palm Springs. Around 1948, she recalls, "He said, 'Beverly, you go over to Borrego and we'll send all these people from Palm Springs who think it's getting too big'—and this was in the late '40s, and it was already too busy for them—'and we'll send them all to Borrego to begin again pioneering in the warmth and the fragile desert feeling.' So I was on the entertainment committee, doing barbecues and planning Jeep rides and horseback rides."[16] The company brought in prospective investors by car, and even sometimes by plane to visit the valley.[17]

CATHERINE STRAND

The Borrego Springs Company sales office, circa 1947. The building still stands.

The Borrego Springs tract was divided into eleven smaller units. First to go on sale were units A and B, along Country Club Road, and along the great loop of Verbena Drive. A week later, unit C, northeast of Christmas Circle, was also placed on the market. Within a year, D and E followed. By 1952 the final unit, K, was on

Borrego Springs from the air, 1953.

the market, and the first houses had been built in unit G. The smallest lots on the tract were still over one-half acre; the estate lots were at least two or three acres each.

While sales of lots continued as each new unit opened, the number of houses built remained small. Many of the lots were sold to speculators who only wanted to hold them for resale when prices went up. During 1954, only twenty-two new homes were built in Borrego Springs. In 1959, thirty-four homes were built, with twenty-six more added in 1960.

The business district around Christmas Circle also developed slowly, yet by November of 1950 Burnand and his partners could boast: "The modernistic Christmas Circle shopping center is operating in full swing and includes the following stores and services: A large Supermarket carrying fresh meats and produce, a first-rate Union Oil Station, a new Drug Store with prescription service and fountain, a fine Physician, a United States Post Office, a Yarn and Knit shop, a Variety Store and a Liquor store. There has been completed in the industrial section a plumbing shop, construction camp, malt shops and restaurants, lumber and builders yard, construction and contracting offices, repair yard, mechanics shops and facilities, to name but a few....

BORREGO SUN

A Borrego Springs billboard along Highway 395 in San Diego County, 1957.

"The future holds many houses to be built and businesses to be started.... A well-run Chamber of Commerce, Kiwanis Club, American Legion, Masonic Lodge and Community Association daily solve civic problems and co-ordinate social advancement.

"All these dreams have become reality in four short years. The advantage of complete planning from the embryo stage insures retention of natural desert beauty. With our progress continuing at the same pace, Borrego Springs is destined to become the finest desert community in the United States."[18]

Telephone service first reached the Borrego Valley in August, 1947, via the El Centro exchange. There were just four phones to start with. Virginia DeMarais recalled: "This was a seventeen-mile line from Ocotillo Wells to Borrego. To call, we had to first listen on the line, then crank the phone for the operator. Each subscriber had a different combination of rings, ours being one long and one short ring—Number 8....

"It was very interesting when we had crank phones; if you wanted to know what was happening in the community, all you had to do was lift the receiver. And also, everyone else could listen in on your conversations!"[19]

Bev Kuhrts adds: "Every time someone would hear that crank, everyone would pick up the receiver to hear who you were going to talk to, or when you were going to go to town, and it was so funny because no one could ever go to town without everybody knowing about it and calling them again and saying, 'Oh, if you're going to town would you pick me up...' whatever. You'd spend most of your time not picking up what you were going to get but shopping for everyone else."[20]

> **"...if you wanted to know what was happening in the community, all you had to do was lift the receiver."**
>
> ***Virginia DeMarais***

In January, 1952, Borrego's entire telephone directory was published in the *Sun*:

Desert Lodge (Kuhrts)	1
DuVall's General Store	2
Borrego School	3
Borrego Springs Tract Office	4
Borrego Land & Development Co.	5
Middlesworth Union Oil Station	6
Hugh Woods' Market Spot	7
Hacienda Borrego Motel (DeMarais)	8
Borrego Village Motel (Jacobs)	9
Borrego Desert Resort (Hoberg's)	10
Borrego Desert Resort	11
Quonset Hut/Borrego Freight Lines	12
Airport	13
Benson Tours	14
Lindberg's Borrego Pharmacy	15
Circle S Liquor Store	17
Martinez Construction Company	18
Borrego Farms (DiGiorgio)	19
Anza Desert State Park	

(Number 16 was still available...if you hurry.)

AUTHOR'S COLLECTION

Borrego Springs Company vice president Fred Marlow and other dignitaries break ground for the Borrego Springs Desert Club in 1948.

The old party line was replaced with dial phones in July, 1956. There were over one hundred phones in the valley by then. Borrego's new prefix was ROckwell 7, but it was not until 1989 that residents had to dial the 767 prefix for local calls.

Television reception in the valley was haphazard in the 1950s, and even the *Sun* was forced to admit, "The TV signal you get in Borrego is largely a matter of luck. Some do, and some don't."[21] In 1953, one of the few stations that came in fairly regularly was KIVA in Yuma, which broadcast only in the evening (but they did run "Captain Video"). Finally in 1963, cable television service became available, via a microwave antenna on Toro Peak.

In 1953, A. A. Burnand and his partners dissolved the original Borrego Springs Land and Development Company, with Burnand, Paul Grafe and Lawrence Barker each retaining a share of the unsold lands. At the end of 1954, Grafe and Barker's three thousand acres were bought out by James Copley, the DiGiorgio Fruit Corporation, and Texas oilman William Black. The new owners then formed their own partnership with A. A. Burnand, Kiva Associates, which controlled a total of six thousand acres in and around the townsite. "With the backing of such men as DiGiorgio, Black and Copley," Burnand told the *Sun*, "and with the diversified experience and abilities of these men, there can be no question about the future of Borrego."[22]

In the coming years, Jim Copley (1916-1973) and DiGiorgio president Robert DiGiorgio (1911-1991) would become major players in the development of Borrego. "Jim just fell in love with Borrego and decided this was the place for him to expand his love," Bev Kuhrts says.[23] Copley was then president, and after 1959 the only stockholder, in The Copley Press, which owned more than a dozen newspapers in California and Illinois, including both the *San Diego Union* and the San Diego *Evening Tribune*.

BORREGO SUN

A rare photo of Borrego Springs' biggest backers and promoters in 1955, showing (left to right) Bud Kuhrts, A. A. Burnand, Jr., Jim Copley, Robert DiGiorgio, and Jack Benson.

Robert DiGiorgio also "had a tremendous love for the valley," Bud Kuhrts recalled, adding, "He was very optimistic, quick and creative, a real sparkplug."[24] A nephew of DiGiorgio founder Joseph DiGiorgio, Bob DiGiorgio joined the family business in 1937 and became president in 1962. Under his leadership, the company went from agriculture to large-scale real estate development. Eventually he became not just a partner, but a son-in-law of A. A. Burnand when he married Burnand's stepdaughter, Pat Kuhrts, in 1964.[25]

CATHERINE STRAND

Robert Ransom, president of the Borrego Springs Company.

The Borrego Springs Company was also dissolved about the same time as the development company, though Harrison Baker and Fred Marlow remained active in valley affairs into the 1960s. To take its place, Bud Kuhrts and Jack Benson formed the Borrego Valley Associates in the fall of 1953. Harry LeClaire, sales manager for the former company, and his associate, Fred Woods, both came over to the new firm, which announced it would "dedicate itself to a planned program of development of the entire tract."[26]

Borrego Valley Associates held the exclusive sales contract for all the local tracts throughout the rest of the decade. In 1960, the firm was sold to the Clair W. Burgener Company of San Diego, with James Murphy taking over the management of the local office.

The growth of Borrego Springs during its first fifteen years was slow. From a population of only ninety in 1940, the area had grown to nearly six hundred residents in 1950, with most of the increase in the previous three years.[27] But a decade later, census takers counted only 780 people in the Borrego area. Then as now, there were about an equal number of seasonal residents and "snow birds."

While lots sold well in the early years, less than twenty percent of them had houses built on them by 1960. Philip Curti, who studied the development of the Borrego Valley in the early 1950s for his master's thesis, noted, "The people who have built homes in the valley are, in the main, retired or semi-retired from business, excluding those who find occupation directly or indirectly concerned with agricultural activity, or who manage the small shops of the business center."[28]

"Realtor Fred Woods feels that most of the absentee landowners are interested in the valley only as an investment and have no plans to improve their lots," the *Borrego Sun* reported in 1961.[29]

Borrego's slow growth has always been the subject of debate. A 1961 summary of Borrego's progress in the *Sun* notes, "Patrick Nolan, Chamber of Commerce manager, cites two points of view on Borrego's growth. He said one group hopes for a speed-up in development and business opportunities. Another group fears that more growth will bring an end to the peace and quiet of the desert community, he said."[30]

It is a debate that still continues.

AGRICULTURE

Agriculture remained the mainstay of Borrego's economy throughout the 1940s and 1950s. The largest operation was the DiGiorgio Fruit Corporation's Borrego Farms. By 1950, DiGiorgio already had more than one thousand acres of vineyards in the north end of the valley, along either side of DiGiorgio Road. By 1957 that figured reached its peak at over twenty-five hundred acres under cultivation.

The early challenges faced by Joseph DiGiorgio and his men after they began developing their ranch in 1945 were described by NBC radio correspondent Henry Schacht in a 1951 broadcast: "Dick Wittman, Wes Harris and Bob DiGiorgio told me of the problems that were faced and conquered, when I visited the ranch. The first question was water. Streams in the surrounding mountains, all flowing or percolating into the Borrego desert, indicated a large pool of underground water. Test drillings located water sometimes as close as thirty feet to the surface. What's more, it comes to the surface at a temperature of eighty-eight degrees—ideal for irrigation. The next step was to make soil analyses. The scientists found that the sand of Borrego was interlaid with strips of silt and that gypsum would be the only fertilizer needed....

> **"1948 was another year of working hard, figuring out the unfamiliar problems of farming the desert and spending more money."**
>
> ***Reporter Henry Schacht***

"Now the stage was set for the attack on the desert. The floor of Borrego Valley is by no means level. Furthermore, the untouched desert supports a fairly thick growth of ocotillo, sage, creosote bush, and other desert plants, all with sturdy roots reaching down to the moisture below. These were cut down with axes and burned. Then the Bechtel Corporation was hired with its giant earth-moving equipment to smooth out the prospective vineyards. Gradually the job progressed. Right behind the earthmovers came the well drillers and the pipe layers.

"Work now had been underway for nearly a year. The spring of '46 saw the first grape plantings. By this time windbreaks were being planted with tamarisk trees, the tree that lives naturally in the arid sections of Australia. Forty-five miles of windbreaks are planted now, three thousand trees, all over forty feet high, making a splendid break against the spring gales.

"But in '46 the trees were only spindly seedlings, and the grapes had to go in. So around every small vine were placed two pieces of box shook to block the wind. The trouble was not enough men were

BORREGO SUN

Worker housing on the DiGiorgio Ranch in the 1950s.

available to place the shook. That year, too, when the winds came, they completely destroyed many of the vines. One block of 250 acres was abandoned. Then jackrabbits, who had never had it so good before, collected by the thousands to feed on the young vines. They ate fifty per cent of the vines in some sections. By the end of the season, less than one-third of the vines planted had survived.

"Nevertheless, 1946 marked the turning point. By the next year the windbreaks started to take hold. Fences had been put up to keep out the rabbits...[and] the grapes were being replanted with rootings from a nursery on the ranch. By the fall of 1947 half of the grapes planted had come through....

"1948 was another year of working hard, figuring out the unfamiliar problems of farming the desert and spending more money. So was 1949, except that for what was now more than two million dollars, Mr. DiGiorgio saw ten carloads of grapes come off his Borrego ranch. Nineteen-fifty started the payoff. Thirty percent of the vines were then in their fourth year. One hundred and forty thousand packages of grapes, mostly Thompson Seedless, were shipped from Borrego under the Verbena brand. Hitting the eastern markets the second week of June, they grossed over $750,000, their only competition coming from Coachella Valley. Packed in the field in Borrego,

BORREGO SUN

Packing grapes in the DiGiorgio packing house, circa 1955.

precooled on the ranch, then rushed by refrigerator trucks the 100 miles to Brawley where they went into reefers, the grapes were in the hands of New York housewives one week after they were picked.... "[31]

Like A. A. Burnand, Joseph DiGiorgio not only saw the possibilities of the Borrego Valley, but had the persistence to make those possibilities come alive. But unlike Burnand, DiGiorgio did not live to see his work completed. He died in 1951, and the leadership of the DiGiorgio Fruit Company eventually passed to his nephew, Robert DiGiorgio.

The DiGiorgio Company eventually sank nearly twenty wells to irrigate their crops. They also built bunk houses for single men, family apartments, and mess halls for their employees, a large packing house and cooling plant (which still stand), and various other facilities. Much of the work force was seasonal. Many of them also worked in the vast DiGiorgio vineyards in the San Joaquin Valley. In 1952, more than six hundred workers were needed to harvest, pack and ship 160,000 boxes of table grapes.

DiGiorgio grew several varieties of grapes, but the largest acreage was always reserved for Thompson Seedless grapes. In 1954,

DiGiorgio had 850 acres of Thompsons, versus 250 acres of Cardinals and just fifty acres each of Red Malagas and Ribiers. They also raised potatoes, asparagus, peaches, plums and a few dates, and experimented with other crops, including onions and garlic.

Borrego Farms was originally managed by Wes Harris and Dick Wittman. Harris had been with DiGiorgio since 1930 and remained active in valley affairs for many years after he left the firm in 1951. Wittman continued on as manager until 1954 when Stu Haseltine took over and managed the ranch through the end of the decade.

DiGiorgio's efforts soon attracted other growers to the Borrego Valley. In the late 1940s, John Kovacevich, another San Joaquin viticulturist, bought seven hundred acres adjoining DiGiorgio's vineyards. He sold out in 1954. The Buerkle brothers, Bill and Wes, also returned from the San Joaquin Valley in the late 1940s to start a local vineyard. By 1957, eight growers had thirty-five hundred acres of grapes in the valley. DiGiorgio had the lion's share with nearly twenty-five hundred acres, but there was also the Hoppe Ranch, Jura Farms, Jack Marovich, the Seely Ranch, the Earl Fruit Company, Leon Campbell and the Buerkle brothers' Flying M Ranch.[32]

Borrego continued to live up to its reputation as the home of early grapes, beating the market every year from 1950 to 1957. DiGiorgio usually made its first shipments in late May, about a week ahead of the Coachella and Imperial Valley growers and about six weeks ahead of their San Joaquin Valley vineyards. In 1959 the Flying M Ranch made the earliest shipment in valley history, trucking out their first grapes on May 19. The yield in Borrego was much smaller than in the San Joaquin Valley, perhaps two-and-a-half tons per acre versus six to nine tons per acre up north, but higher prices at the start of the season offset the lower yields. On June 15, 1953, for example, DiGiorgio grapes from Borrego were selling in New York at $12.50 a box. By July 1, as other growers hit the market, the price was down to $3.27 a box.[33]

DiGiorgio harvested its last Borrego grapes in 1966. As California's largest grape growers, Caesar Chavez's United Farm Workers made a special effort to unionize DiGiorgio's employees, and with such a short picking season for grapes, the DiGiorgios feared that a harvest-time strike could be devastating, so they decided to abandon the grape business and shift their efforts to real estate development. By 1969, the last DiGiorgio vineyards in Central California had been sold. The last Borrego Valley grapes were shipped from the Seely Ranch around that time.

While grapes dominated the valley throughout the 1950s, a variety of other crops was tried by ranchers large and small. Some never got beyond the experimental stage. In 1954, the crop acreage in the valley was:

Grapes	2,360 acres
Alfalfa	1,000 acres
Cotton	285 acres
Broom corn	225 acres
Asparagus	220 acres
Squash	77 acres
Grapefruit	60 acres
Corn	60 acres
Tomatoes	50 acres
Crenshaw melons	40 acres
Dates	35 acres
Sweet Potatoes	30 acres
Flowers	20 acres
Peaches	20 acres
Black-eyed beans	16 acres
String beans	16 acres
Tangerines	15 acres
Okra	5 acres
Garlic	2 acres
Onions	1 acre[34]

One of the early, successful vegetable ranches was the Borrego Springs Co-Op Farms, founded in 1947 by George Shintaku and the Uyeda brothers. The partners leased several parcels in the valley and

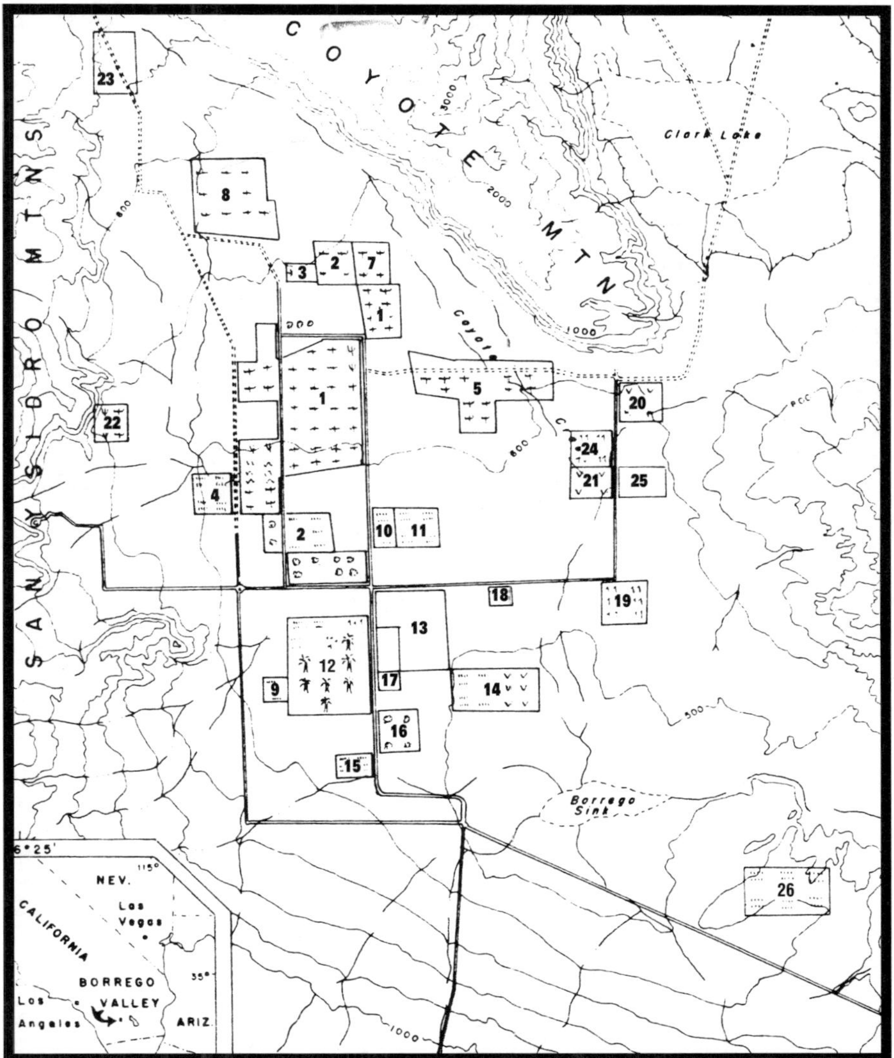

1 DiGiorgio's Borego Farms (1,940 acres; grapes, asparagus)
2 Kovacevich (600 acres; grapes, cotton)
3 Fortiner's Glad Ranch (160 acres; flowers)
4 Hauser (160 acres; alfalfa)
5 Lynn Ranch (700 acres; grapes, alfalfa)
7 Marovich (160 acres; grapes, tangerines)
8 Mirasol Ranch (720 acres; grapes)
9 Walters (40 acres; alfalfa)
10 Baker (80 acres; alfalfa, beans)
11 Castrell (160 acres; alfalfa)
12 Ensign Ranch (1,040 acres; dates, hogs)
13 Burnand (500 acres; alfalfa, cotton)
14 Kosky Ranch (320 acres; alfalfa)
15 Grimm (60 acres; alfalfa)
16 Jacobs (146 acres; cotton)
17 Ostrom (20 acres; no crops)
18 Audette (40 acres; broom corn)
19 Simas (160 acres; no crops)
20 Seely (208 acres; grapes, vegetables)
21 Harris & Fortiner (108 acres; sweet potatoes)
22 Riverall Ranch (no crops)
23 De Anza Ranch (no crops)
24 Zeutzius (no crops)
25 Pederson (no crops)
26 Wear (alfalfa)

G. PHILIP CURTI

The major ranches in the Borrego Valley in 1954.

BORREGO SUN

The farmlands spread out across the upper end of the Borrego Valley, circa 1950.

planted tomatoes, eggplant, peppers, cantaloupes and sweet corn. In 1954-55, Shintaku also managed the Lynn Ranch, which had early vegetables and more than four hundred acres of alfalfa. Shintaku's son, Leroy, recently recalled, "My family arrived in the valley in the late '40s. There were five families of Japanese-American descent that came to start over after the relocation camps of World War II.... We lived on the Co-op farm and grew tomatoes, melons, corn, and any vegetables we needed for everyday use.... We lived in the barracks left by the military. The barracks were partitioned for rooms, the kids' room, parents' bedroom, and the kitchen-living room-dining room. We used a swamp cooler in the summer and a large wood-burning potbelly stove in the winter....

"Our parents worked every day in the fields, and in the packing shed during the harvest. My cousin, Jimmy Uyeda, and I started driving tractors in the fields by the fourth grade. We were paid for this, but I can't remember how much. We worked from 7 a.m. to 11 a.m., then went to school from 12 p.m. to 5 p.m. Sometimes we worked after school for a couple of hours....

"In the beginning, we were taking the produce to Los Angeles ourselves. After the produce was packed for market, my dad would take the load to the Los Angeles produce market....

"I think back about growing up in Borrego and believe there wasn't a better place for me to have spent my childhood."[35]

BORREGO SUN

George Shintaku (right) inspects some of the sweet corn crop with James Dalles, the new owner of the Lynn Ranch, 1955.

Writing in 1954, George Shintaku recalled his early experiences as a Borrego Valley farmer: "In 1947 a handful of farmers at the Glad Ranch, DiGiorgio Farms, Kovacevich Ranch, Ensign Ranch, and the Co-op Farms were in the throes of a pioneering dilemma....

"Labor, communication, transportation, supplies, parts and repairs are all vital to successful farming. All are being made more accessible today. Five years ago when it was necessary to order seed or replace a broken machine part, the nearest phone was Ocotillo [Wells]. Many times the trip to Ocotillo was made and the phone call completed only to find that El Centro and Escondido were still growing, too. [...and couldn't supply what was needed.]

"I think back about growing up in Borrego and believe there wasn't a better place for me to have spent my childhood."

Leroy Shintaku

"When Yaqui Pass was the only roundabout way of getting to Brawley and El Centro, many truckers just weren't interested in getting our produce out of the valley and to a market.

"Today, you couldn't ask for a better road than the new cut-off at the [Desert] Lodge....

"Obtaining parts and repairs is still, however, one of our most difficult problems. A few ranches today have their own machine shops, where a broken part is mended, but for the most part, the Borrego farmer has to make many costly trips out of the valley for repairs and replacements on machinery. Many times the round trip of 120 miles has to be made to simply replace a bolt worth nine cents. You can't show farm profit when the cost to do the job is prohibitive. But some day, someone will have a good machine and repair shop for the farmers of the valley....

"Sam [Fortiner] and I agreed that the good old days were not always good...they were trial-and-error and learn-by-experience days. And we still have much to learn.

"You can't fight the weather, but you can learn to live with it. You can't post a sign on your farm saying 'Rabbits, gophers, aphids...Keep Out.' But we can and must work together as valley farmers, toward their extinction....

"Borrego farmers still have their trials and tribulations, they still make errors, but we are beginning to get the 'feel' of farming in the desert and, coupled with our knowledge gained the hard way, we are learning to meet the challenges of farming with confidence."

George Shintaku

"Borrego farmers still have their trials and tribulations, they still make errors, but we are beginning to get the 'feel' of farming in the desert and, coupled with our knowledge gained the hard way, we are learning to meet the challenges of farming with confidence."[36]

The Lynn Ranch in the northeast part of the valley along Henderson Canyon Road was noted for its vegetables, though they also grew a lot of alfalfa. Its founder, J. J. Lynn, was a Midwestern insurance executive and a leader in the Self-Realization Fellowship spiritual movement. "He came out here with the thought that if he bought enough land and had the right help, which was the Shintaku family, that he could raise fresh vegetables and produce for all of the

Self-Realization people [across the United States]," Bev Kuhrts recalls. "So that was his big quest, and he got himself really involved in it, and he had money to spend. And I think he, unfortunately, died way before his time; he died very suddenly, and right in the middle of all this wonderful development."[37]

The Lynn Ranch was one of several farms in the valley that maintained its own worker housing. Leroy Shintaku recalls that by the time his father took over the management of the ranch in the mid-1950s, "...the Bracero worker program allowed us to bring Mexican nationals into the U. S. to work on the farm. Prior to that, all of the workers were illegal workers from Mexico. Most of the workers would come back every year. Under the Bracero program the workers lived in large dorms, had separate cooking, showers, bathrooms, and laundry facilities.... The [Lynn] farm also had a baseball diamond and movies on Saturday night for the workers.... There were baseball games between the Lynn farms, DiGiorgio, and the town guys."[38]

BORREGO SUN

Sam Fortiner, checking out the gladiolas in his greenhouse, 1966.

Sam Fortiner, another well-known valley rancher, acquired his first 160 acres in Borrego in 1944 and drilled his first well in 1945. Fortiner's "Glad Ranch" was unique in Borrego; his principal crop was gladiolas. Like other valley farmers, Fortiner's goal was to "beat the market." He had been growing "glads" at Vista with his partner, Wilson Vinson, since before the war and first visited Borrego at the invitation of Harry Woods' son, Win, a California Highway Patrol officer on the San Diego coast. "I think this was in November," Fortiner recalls, "and it was one of those beautiful, nice, sunny, calm days; nice and warm, just a realtor's dream come true."[39]

BORREGO SUN

The packing house on the DiGiorgio Ranch in the mid-1950s. The building, long abandoned, still stands.

Fortiner was sold, and he and his partner began developing their desert ranch. Later, when Vinson wanted out, Fortiner decided to stay in Borrego, and Vinson kept their Vista operation. By the mid-1950s Fortiner had about thirty acres in flowers, mostly gladiolas, but he also grew other varieties. Fortiner rotated his fields with various row crops, including string beans, squash and even a little okra.

Like other Borrego farmers, Fortiner had to learn from experience. The desert climate was the major threat. "It seemed like we'd go three bad years and then a good year," he says, "then another three bad ones, and then a good one. So we decided we'd whip that, and we built plastic-covered houses. That wasn't too bad. We grew some beautiful stuff underneath them, and we could get that in early, because it was warmer inside. We'd be cutting flowers in January. And when a cold night would come along we'd have heaters in them, and then our water in our well comes out at about seventy-eight degrees, and we'd turn the sprinklers on and there'd just be a fog bank inside those houses; didn't take but just a few minutes."

The summer heat was another threat: "We had a big cold storage plant and we'd put all the bulbs into storage. You'd dig 'em out of the ground, clean 'em, disinfect 'em, and put them into cold storage. Then when you start planting you can rotate them, take some out at the first of the month, then some more on the tenth, and that would spread out your cutting season."[40]

In 1955, Philip Curti noted that Fortiner's ranch "has probably proved to be the most profitable of the smaller ranches of the Borrego Valley. Besides the packing shed and the ranch house, there are two small wooden houses for the Mexican laborers. The labor force usually consists of six men who are hired on an eighteen-month contract, there being sufficient work to employ these men throughout the year, and they work under the direction of an overseer who occupies a somewhat more pretentious house."[41]

Cutting season for the gladiolas began around New Year's and continued until about the first of March. The flowers were packed a dozen to a bunch, and about ten dozen to a can. In 1958 the *Sun* reported that Fortiner was expecting his biggest harvest ever, some 100,000 dozen.

BORREGO SUN

Jack Russell shows off some of his grapefruit crop, 1959.

In the 1960s, the public taste began turning away from gladiolas and other "big funeral flowers," as Fortiner jokingly calls them. Like other farmers, he also began to see more and more South American crops hitting the American market. So Fortiner started to move into citrus, primarily lemons, and by the mid-1970s was out of the flower business.

The valley's first cash crop, alfalfa, continued to be popular into the 1950s. As late as 1954 there were still about one thousand acres growing in Borrego. A. A. Burnand had several hundred acres, and Jack Benson and Dick Wear both harvested crops in the early 1950s. "Alfalfa" Bill Baker had another eighty acres on his Rancho Cali-Borrego.

Beginning in 1953, A. A. Burnand's youngest son, Perry (1926-1979), made a new attempt at growing cotton in the valley, and by 1954 had more than 250 acres under cultivation. Bill Baker later followed up with another thirty acres on the Rancho Cali-Borrego.

As in the 1930s, this was the only cotton grown in San Diego County, and their crop had to be hauled to gins in Imperial Valley for processing.

In 1955, Perry Burnand turned over his cotton operation to the new Anza Land Company, which he had formed with the Buerkle brothers. The new partners leased several large ranches in the valley, beginning with A. A. Burnand's "Fun Farm," and later adding the old Lynn Ranch and three hundred acres on the Ensign Ranch. Perry Burnand served as general manager of the operation, with Bill Bailey as superintendent and Wes Harris as foreman.

BORREGO SUN

DiGiorgio manager Stu Haseltine (right) displays some of the 1958 grape harvest to a local visitor.

In addition to its cotton acreage, the Anza Land Company grew alfalfa, grapes, asparagus and celery. In 1959 they also began a feed cattle operation, bringing in sixteen hundred head. The cotton harvests continued until the winter of 1966-67, when all the fields in the valley were destroyed by a pink bollworm.

Citrus began to make its appearance in the mid-1950s. Jack Marovich was one of the first local ranchers to go in for citrus, beginning with grapefruit in 1953. By 1954 Marovich had twenty-nine acres of citrus, including oranges, lemons and tangerines. The Lynn Ranch also had ten experimental citrus acres by 1954. Because the trees take several years to come to bearing, the valley's first commercial grapefruit crop was not shipped until 1958. It was only when grapes went out in the 1960s that citrus farming really took hold in the valley.

The historic old Ensign Ranch continued to be a good producer into the 1950s. Dates remained its best-known crop. They had sixteen hundred trees producing nine different varieties: Khadrawy, Halawy, Saidy, Hayany, Tazizoot, Khustawy, Zahidi, Thoory and the always popular Deglet Noor. In 1957, after more than thirty years, the family finally sold out to a group of Eastern investors headed by Patrick Nolan, a former Detroit lumber dealer, who came to take charge of the operation. Nolan and his partners briefly renamed the ranch Nolacres, but in 1959 the Ensign name was revived. The Ensigns' longtime manager, Tom Davis (1911-1997), stayed on to work for the new owners. In 1959 Patrick Nolan noted, "Since first planted, the [date] grove has been maintained on an 'organic growth' basis. No commercial fertilizer has been applied to the soil nor have any poisonous spray or insecticides been used on the trees or fruit in past years. This program will be continued so that only naturally grown, tree-ripened fruit from a grove fertilized by return of organic materials to the soil will be produced."[42]

Nolan and his partners sold out in 1962 for a reported $1,400,000. The new owners planned a residential development called Borrego Springs Park, which opened in 1964, and a golf course at Club Circle. Once again, Tom Davis stayed on to work with the new owners and became general manager of the Borrego Springs Park Community Services District. He and his wife Bernice remained in Borrego until 1991, when the old ranch was sold to the Cameron Brothers.

NEW ROADS

Both the agricultural and residential development in Borrego required better highway access into and out of the valley. Three new roads received most of the attention in the early years, though only two of them were ever built.

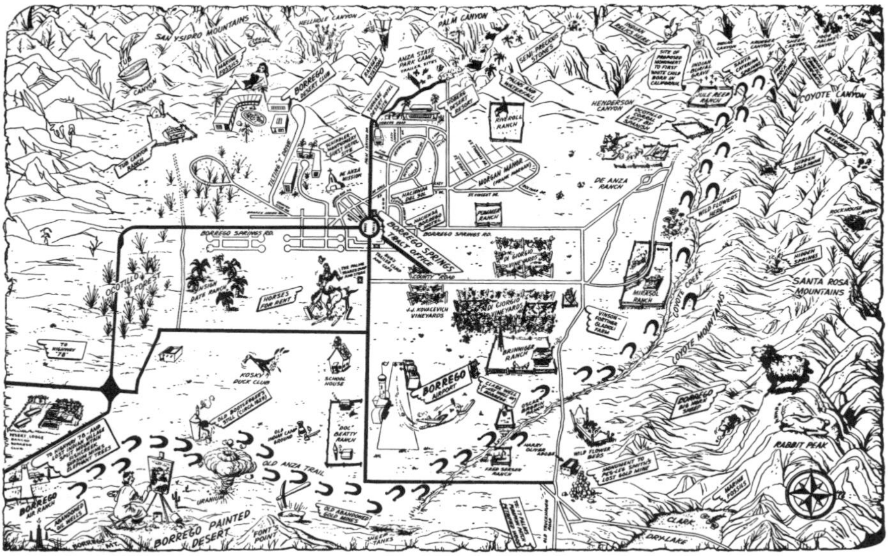

AUTHOR'S COLLECTION

This "fun map" of the Borrego Valley was put out by the Borrego Springs Company in 1949 and used to promote the area for a number of years.

The idea of a road down the mountain from Ranchita through Culp Valley dates back to before 1920, but it was not until the early 1950s that plans seriously began to take shape. A. A. Burnand lobbied the State Park Commission long and hard to secure the necessary right-of-way down the mountain. Though park staff in Sacramento opposed the plan, in 1953 the State Park Commission, including former Borrego Springs honorary mayor Leo Carrillo, gave the proposal the green light.

County prison camp crews began work on the 12.9-mile road during the summer of 1954. An Honor Camp was built in Ranchita, and all the initial work was done from the top down. It was not until the final year or two of the project that a second construction crew started work from the bottom upward. By 1957, about half the right-of-way had been roughed out, but that only brought the crews to the hardest part of the job. "It's slow, rough going right now," Construction Superintendent James Reed told the *Borrego Sun* in April of 1957. "They're cutting through solid rock and right now are working on a cliff 150 feet high."

Throughout the late '50s and early '60s, completion of the Montezuma Valley Road always seemed to be "just two or three years away." In the end, the job took nearly ten years. On June 24, 1964, nearly one thousand people braved the 114-degree heat to watch the ribbon cutting on what Jim Copley called "the glass elevator" down the mountainside. That same fall, the county honor crews began work on the second important new road to the valley, the Borrego-Salton Seaway, which was completed in 1968.

The founding of Borrego Springs also revived the old proposal of a road through Coyote Canyon, an idea that dates back at least as far as 1920. Supporters, including the Borrego Springs Chamber of Commerce, even managed to get the road on San Diego County's master plan of highways in the mid-1950s, but, despite more than half a century of debate, the road has never been built.

Within the valley, the birth of Borrego Springs also prompted the construction of a curving grid of residential streets. "Roads have been named for desert plants and flowers, and for famous old Western cattle ranch brands," one of the first sales brochures notes. Christmas Circle was named in honor of the Christmas-time birth of

BORREGO SUN

Cutting the ribbon to open the Montezuma Grade in 1964 are Borrego's honorary mayor, actor Gale Gordon, Jim Copley, Miss Borrego Springs Marilyn Druliner and County Supervisor Robert Cozens.

Salvador Ignacio Linares in Coyote Canyon during the Anza Expedition in 1775.[43] In 1952, construction began on a fountain in the center of the circle as a memorial to Joseph DiGiorgio. It was removed in 1985 when Christmas Circle was renovated.

MOTELS AND RESORTS

The local tourism industry also benefited from easier access in and out of Borrego and, along with agriculture, formed the backbone of the valley's economy.

Though not the first resort in the valley, (the Desert Lodge preceding it by nearly a decade) Hoberg's Desert Resort was the biggest and most important resort motel in the early days of Borrego Springs. The Hoberg family had been in the vacation business since the 1880s, when they opened Hoberg's Lake County Resort on their family ranch in Northern California. In 1933, three Hoberg brothers, Frank, George and Paul, took over the family business.

Hoberg's Lake County was strictly a summertime resort, and for many years the brothers toyed with the idea of opening a second, winter resort, at a warmer location. In 1946, they met A. A. Burnand, who had just the spot in mind.

Burnand introduced George and Frank Hoberg to the Borrego Valley (Paul having passed away by then), and sold them on the idea of establishing their second resort here. They selected a seventy-two-acre site on the west side of the valley, right along the edge of the state park, with a view down across the valley. Construction began in the early months of 1947, and the first ten rooms of "Hoberg's Desert Resort" opened for business on New Year's Day, 1948.

BORREGO SUN

Hoberg's Desert Resort was the pride of Borrego Springs in the early 1950s.

Work on the resort continued into 1948, and a more festive opening was held that November. "That was a big blast when that opened up," Sam Fortiner recalls. "They had a big party up there. It was well done; the rooms were not much of anything, they were kind of crude, pretty rough, but for just a weekend or a couple of days, why they were sufficient. And the food was good and their bar was wet. And the pool was wet. It was really the spot at that time."[44]

Eleven more rooms were added in 1949, and Hoberg's stayed open all summer. Eventually there were sixty rooms, an Olympic-size swimming pool, tennis courts, a coffee shop, a beauty parlor and a private airstrip. Frank Hoberg would sometimes fly down in his own Bonanza aircraft. The Hobergs had originally hoped to move their staff back and forth between their two resorts from season to season, but that plan did not work out.

The first local managers were Jack and Ella Benson. Jack Benson had previously spent eighteen years about as far away from the desert as one can get—working for the United States Fish and Wildlife Service in Alaska. He had met his future wife while on vacation in 1945, while she was working at the historic Desert Inn in Palm Springs. The couple came to Borrego in 1948 and managed Hoberg's off and on until the beginning of the 1950 season, Phil Ellis taking the helm for part of 1949. O. M. "Ollie" Merrill followed, serving until the Hobergs sold out in 1951.

The ownership of the resort changed many times during the 1950s. Frank Hoberg died of a heart attack in December, 1948. In 1950, the ownership passed to Paul's widow, Mildred Hoberg. She sold the resort to Richard Bennett and Nora Craig in 1951, who renamed it the Borrego Desert Resort, and again in 1953 the Borrego Palms Resort. The next owner was Helen Eder of Los Angeles, who sold the resort to Roy Riner of San Diego in 1954. In 1956 he sold to the Del Thurber Construction Company of San Diego, who sold it less than a year later to an investment group headed by A. C. Schoultz of San Antonio, Texas. After that, the ownership settled down for a few years.

Robert C. Burns handled the day-to-day management of the resort for the new owners. On the evening of April 22, 1958, he heard a strange sound upstairs, and rushed outside to find flames bursting out of the roof of the main building. Within a short time, the building was completely destroyed by fire. According to the *Borrego Sun*: "The combined efforts of hundreds of volunteers and a sudden, last-minute shift of wind prevented the flames from spreading to either [of] the hotel's seventy dwelling units on either side of the main building or to other nearby homes in the valley.

"The roaring blaze, which lit up the entire floor of the valley, was finally extinguished with the aid of three fire trucks from the State Division of Forestry which were called in from Julian, thirty-five miles away.

"Damage was estimated unofficially at $200,000. The fire completely destroyed the main building which housed the dining room, lobby, coffee shop, cocktail lounge, ballroom, recreation area and several offices....

"[T]he blaze started...when a [gas] hot water tank exploded on the second floor of the hotel above the beauty shop.... The flames spread quickly and their brilliant glow attracted nearly every resident of the valley to the scene.... The flames, fed by a brisk west wind,

BORREGO SUN

The results of the disastrous Hoberg's fire in 1958.

threatened a number of homes to the east of the hotel. Volunteers wet down these danger spots with garden hoses until a sudden shift of the wind eliminated this threat.

"Other volunteers with hoses which were rushed to the scene from DiGiorgio's Borrego Farms, fought valiantly and successfully to save the cabanas and other living areas on either side of the main building."[45]

The Borrego Palms fire was a devastating blow, but Schoultz and his partners rallied and reopened barely a month later, on May 24, 1958, with the offices, lobby and coffee shop moved to a small building near the swimming pool. Construction of a new main building began that October, and the new Borrego Palms Resort was ready to open in time for the beginning of the 1959 season.

In the mid-1960s the resort closed, reopening in 1966 as The Palms School for Exceptional Children, which operated there for more than a decade. In 1977 it was sold to a new owner who reopened it as a private resort known as Earth Station I. A couple other owners followed before the resort closed up again. It was not until 1994 that the resort was renovated and reopened as The Palms at Indian Head. Today it has rejoined the ranks of Borrego's resort destinations.

Earth Station II

BORREGO SUN

Mr. and Mrs. Ray Freelund watch the walls go up on the new addition at their Stanlund's Motel in 1960.

The early history of the Desert Lodge has already been described in the first chapter. Noel and Ruth Crickmer continued to run their resort until early 1947 when they sold out to the Burnand interests. For much of that year, the entire Desert Lodge was leased by the DiGiorgio Fruit Company, which used the resort for employee housing until the bunkhouses on their ranch were completed. With the sale of the Desert Lodge in 1947, Noel and Ruth Crickmer moved up to the old Fred Lanz ranch in Tub Canyon and announced plans for a new, more rustic resort, the Tub Canyon Guest Ranch, which the Crickmers ran until the early 1950s.

Bud Kuhrts then took over the operation of the Lodge for the family, and in 1948 construction began on twelve additional units and a new lobby, which were completed in 1949, along with a swimming pool. The resort was remodeled in 1953, and a "pitch-and-putt" golf course was added across the road, in the little triangle formed as the Yaqui Pass Road curves down to meet Borrego Springs Road. Business was slow in the early days, and limited mostly to the weekends. "We used to talk about throwing nails in the middle of the highway to get people to stop on their way down the hill," Bev Kuhrts jokes.[46]

With his many activities in the valley, Bud Kuhrts soon gave up the day-to-day management of the Desert Lodge and hired resident managers to run the resort. Ollie Merrill was the first, in 1949. Carl and Olga Vogt looked after the place for several years, as did Marty and Wanda Pavletich.

In 1960, the Burnand family sold the Desert Lodge to MACOP, a new corporation formed by James Copley. According to the *Borrego Sun*, "The Lodge facilities consist of a main building with dining room, kitchen, Ocotillo Room and lobby, 19 motel units, a two story residence to the rear of the Lodge, a swimming pool and the Kiva Room, a facility for meetings and private parties."

Copley told the paper: "The reputation of Borrego Springs, San Diego County's desert playground, as one of the nation's finest desert resorts, is being spread far and wide, and this reputation is bringing to Borrego and to San Diego County people from all parts of this country and Canada.

"To preserve and enhance this reputation additional hotel facilities with all the essential accommodations for visitors are a must

BORREGO SUN

The lobby at the Desert Lodge, circa 1960, not long before the resort was renamed La Casa del Zorro.

today in Borrego. The MACOP Corporation has been organized to help meet these needs."[47]

Copley and his partners renamed the resort La Casa del Zorro, and it opened for the 1960 season on October 14, with Bill Plant as the new resident manager. Jim Copley took an active interest in the resort, as he did with all his holdings in Borrego Valley, and by moving his annual Copley Conferences to La Casa del Zorro, he introduced the resort and the valley to newspaper executives and public figures from across the United States. Today, more than sixty years after its founding, La Casa del Zorro is not only the oldest, but the most prestigious, desert resort in the Borrego Valley.

The DeMaraises had been lured to the infant Borrego Springs tract... by a persuasive real estate salesman.

"I thought he [her husband] had lost his mind."

Virginia DeMarais

The first motel "in town" was the Hacienda del Sol, built by Herb Haughton and his wife, Charlotte (Kuhrts) Haughton, late in 1947. Originally, the Hacienda del Sol offered only "cottage" rooms. Haughton sold out around 1950, and it was William Furlong who built most of what we now know as the Hacienda del Sol between 1956 and 1960, when the lobby and adjoining storefronts were added along Palm Canyon Drive. Furlong sold out in the early 1960s.

The next place in town was Bill and Virginia DeMarais' Hacienda Borrego, just north of Christmas Circle on Borrego Springs Road at Cloudy Moon Drive. "We wanted to be near the town, but not in the town," Virginia later recalled, "and in '47 our location was out of town somewhat."[48]

The DeMaraises had been lured to the infant Borrego Springs tract from the Los Angeles area in 1947 by a persuasive real estate salesman. "I thought he had lost his mind," Virginia recalled, when her husband announced his intention to move to the valley. "There were only a few things here, the Desert Lodge, and that was about it."[49]

They began construction of the Hacienda in 1948, with Bill and Virginia doing as much of the work themselves as they could. The eight-room motel was ready for occupancy by the end of summer and had its formal opening on September 18, 1948.

Bill and Virginia DeMarais took an active role in the community from the start, through the Chamber of Commerce, the Kiwanis Club, the Community Church (now the Community United Methodist Church), the Borrego Elementary School and many other projects and organizations. The Borrego Springs Library started in their living room/lobby at the Hacienda Borrego. Bill DeMarais ran the projector for the Kiwanis' outdoor motion picture shows. Virginia was best known as Borrego Springs' official historian, and for nearly forty years wrote her "Do You Recall?" column for the *Borrego Sun*.

The DeMaraises sold the Hacienda Borrego in 1954 to Virginia's parents, Buzz and Virginia Wharton, and they continued to run the motel into the 1960s. Today it is known as the Whispering Sands. Bill DeMarais died in 1982, and Virginia passed away twelve years later.

To serve the growing travel trailer crowd, Jack Benson laid out the Palms Trailer Court in 1948, along Palm Canyon Drive at DiGiorgio Road. When completed in 1949, the park offered full hook-ups, including electricity. There was also a small country store. F. T. Beniteau served as Benson's manager, while Jack and Ella Benson were busy managing Hoberg's Desert Resort and Benson Tours. The park eventually closed, and the site was used for many years as a driving range.

Ray and Thelma Jacobs built the next motel in the valley, the Borrego Village Motel, which opened at the beginning of 1949. It was located two miles north of the Desert Lodge on what was then known as Schoolhouse Road—now Borrego Valley Road. The Jacobses sold out in 1954 to Jack Raney, who hired Mr. and Mrs. Charles Richards to manage the motel for him. Raney added four units in 1956. He died in 1958, and a year later his widow sold the motel to Donald LeRoux of La Jolla. It was sold again in 1961 to Thomas Beadry of Santee. Today the old motel complex serves as employee housing for La Casa del Zorro.

Jack and Bea Shinn opened the Ja-Ca-Bea Motel on Borrego Springs Road around the beginning of 1950. They sold out to Mr. and Mrs. Frank Peck, but the old name survived for many years. Today it is the Mar-Dean Apartments.

The first six units of what is now Stanlund's Resort Inn and Suites were built in 1950 by Roy Guppy, who moved to Borrego with his wife, Harriet, a year later. In 1952 they built a swimming pool, and in 1953 they added five more units to what they simply called Guppy's Motel.

In 1956 the Guppys sold out to L. W. Stanfield and Ray Freelund. Freelund and his wife took over the day-to-day management of the motel, and in 1957 the new owners combined their names to christen their motel Stanlund's. In 1960, they added yet another six units to the motel.

After the sale of the motel, the Guppys moved to Joshua Tree, where Roy Guppy died in 1960 at the age of fifty-six. Ray Freelund eventually acquired full ownership of Stanlund's, which he sold in 1978, three years before his death.

In 1953, Carl and Olga Vogt opened another trailer park, the Lazy V Resort, now known as El Rancho Trailer Park, on two-and-a-half acres on Palm Canyon Drive. The Vogts had been visiting the valley for several years before deciding to throw their lot in with Borrego Springs. Later, they would become the managers of the Desert Lodge.

Further out of town, Ben Audette opened up the Molino Verde Motel in 1956, on the old Doc Beaty homestead across from the airport. Audette also held the lease on the airport in the late 1950s and built the first restaurant there, The Luau, in 1960. He owned both the motel and restaurant until his death in 1969.

The year 1958 marked the opening of the Oasis Motel, built by Mr. and Mrs. Harold Craum. In 1960 construction began nearby on the Desert Sands Park. Mr. and Mrs. Shirley Schroeder were the first managers.

Some of the tourist business spilled over from Borrego Valley to Ocotillo Wells, where about twenty-five families were living by

1951. There were several small tourist stops along the highway there, including Scotty's Desert Resort and Lola LeBard's Ocotillo Wells Inn with its restaurant, service station and tourist cabins.

The first, and as yet only, motel in Ocotillo Wells was the Ironwoods Motel, built in 1957. Much of the original building was destroyed by fire in 1988, but was rebuilt and expanded to twelve units in 1989.

TOURISTS AND WILDFLOWERS

Needless to say, no resort, motel or trailer park brings in the visitors like a good crop of tiny little desert wildflowers. In the 1930s the wildflower tourists came by the hundreds. By the late 1940s, they were coming by the thousands. As it happened, there were some wonderful wildflower years just as Borrego Springs was getting started. "In the early '50s the flowers were fantastic," says Bev Kuhrts. "The entire valley, if you came from any direction, looked like a purple valley, the verbena were that thick. You almost didn't want to walk because you'd crush these gorgeous scenes. Between the verbena and the golden poppies and the white desert lilies, it was just fantastic. We had two or three different years, not in succession, when the flowers were so spectacular...you just can't describe it, it was so fantastic. The entire valley was just a beauty spot, all you could see were the different hues of flowers."[50]

Nineteen forty-nine was a particularly good flower year. The second issue of the *Borrego Sun* (April, 1949) reported: "Cars were crawling bumper to bumper throughout Borrego valley. Some observers claimed the steady stream of cars was a solid mass reaching as far as Ramona."

An unidentified poet captured the scene for the *Ramona Sentinel* in a poem called "I Went to Borrego!"

I went to Borrego to look at the flowers
And breathe desert air of relaxing powers.
I take to the highway on bright Sunday last
And toward peaceful mountains my vision I cast.

Did I say "peaceful," let me make myself clear,
We soon caught a million headed East in low gear,
Cars, trucks and cycles clogged "seventy-eight,"
Turning motoring pleasure to terror or hate.

We crept into Julian, on down the grade,
But the traffic increased instead of to fade;
In Banner they formed long lines for gas,
Had anyone told me I have said truth, alas.

Down Sentenac Canyon, up other side,
Heavens to Betsy, on goes the tide,
Down the Valley as far as you look
Thousands of cars form a dark, snaky crook.

Cars fill the road, both coming and going
Cars line the highway to nigh overflowing,
Cars jammed the village so no one could budge,
For e'en a cold drink a mile I must trudge.

What of the flowers—lovely, I guess,
I never saw them through this awful mess;
A glimpse now and then when some vehicle stalled
Gave my heart a weak beat as the color enthralled.

I was too hot and too harassed to rave,
This fight for survival was just for the brave...[51]

The next big wildflower year was 1952, when 11,799 cars entered the valley over the weekend of April 4-6—almost all of them coming over the winding Yaqui Pass Road. Nineteen fifty-seven was said to be the best wildflower year since 1949. On Sunday, March 17, alone, it was estimated there were ten thousand cars and some thirty thousand people in the valley.

BORREGO SUN

Tourists who braved the heat to attend the 1955 Sun Worshippers Celebration received these certificates from the Borrego Springs Chamber of Commerce.

The springs of 1948 and '49 saw the last revivals of the old Ocotillo Day celebrations, which had begun in 1934. After that the big community celebrations shifted to the fall, at the start of the desert tourist season. Beginning in 1948, Hoberg's, the Desert Lodge, and many of the smaller motels all held annual "start-of-the-season" parties and special events.

In 1955 Borrego Springs began celebrating the opening of the season each October with "Covered Wagon Daze." The biggest draw of the weekend was the Peg Leg Smith Liars Contest, which drew fifteen hundred spectators that year.[52]

The *Borrego Sun* described the festivities planned for the 1957 "Days of the Dons" celebration, as it was called that year: "Borrego's 1957-58 season opens this month with a full schedule of attractions for all types of desert lovers, and even more for those who don't care particularly about the desert but just like their fun in large doses.

"Major event of the month will be the 'Days of the Dons' celebration Oct. 11 through 13. Highlights of this event, for which Borrego residents and business firms will don Spanish dress, will be a major AAU swimming meet, the annual Peg Leg Liars Contest and a Spanish costume dance, all at Borrego Palms Resort.

"The swimming meet, which is expected to attract more than 200 entries from the San Diego and Los Angeles area, will be held in the Resort's Olympic size pool from 10 a.m. to 2 p.m. Oct. 13....

"County Clerk Bud James will again serve as master of ceremonies for the Peg Leg Liars Contest on Saturday night, Oct. 12, at the Resort....

"Prizes in the Liars Contest as well as prizes for the best costumes will be awarded at a costume dance following the tall-tale telling in the ballroom of the Borrego Palms Resort.

"Other events during the celebration will be a square dance at Christmas Circle Friday night, Oct. 11; an early morning horseback ride to Hell Hole Canyon and a nature hike conducted by Dalton Merkel, state park naturalist, Saturday morning, and a kids parade Saturday afternoon."[53]

BORREGO SUN

Harry Oliver (right), poses with pioneer Borego booster Harry Woods at the new Peg Leg Smith Monument in 1960.

In 1958 the Covered Wagon Daze name was revived, and the celebration continued into the 1960s. The 1960 edition featured Borrego's resident television star and Honorary Mayor, Gale Gordon, as master of ceremonies for the Peg Leg contest. Contest founder Harry Oliver was also present to unveil an official state historical landmark plaque in honor of Peg Leg Smith. "This is the happiest moment of my life," Oliver told the crowd. "I have a lump in my throat so big it will take at least two bourbons to wash it down."[54]

In 1966, Covered Wagon Daze was replaced by the Desert Festival, which has been held nearly every year since.

These fall festivals celebrate the return of cooler weather to the desert and the tourists it brings, but for the year 'round visitors and residents in the 1950s, there was also the annual Sun Worshippers Celebration, held at the height of summer each July.

The first Sun Worshippers Celebration was held on July 16, 1955, when hundreds gathered in the 112-degree heat to stage and watch a parade down Palm Canyon Drive and to see Hollywood "starlet" Kathy Marlowe crowned as Borrego's Sun Goddess. The Sun Worshippers parade continued throughout the rest of the decade; 350 people attended the second edition in 1956. The highest temperature recorded for the event was on July 11, 1959, when the mercury topped 114 degrees. This is one early Borrego Springs tradition that for some reason has not survived.

Another part of Borrego's tourist industry is the tour operators, who offer four-wheel-drive treks into the surrounding desert. The first was Benson Tours, founded by Jack and Ella Benson in 1949; Benson also served as the valley's first Willys Jeep dealer. The Bensons eventually sold out, but the firm continued as Benson Tours into the 1960s.

BUSINESSES

Downtown Borrego Springs grew up to serve both the residents and tourists who discovered the Borrego Valley in the late 1940s and early '50s.

The first store in Borrego Springs was the Borrego Mercantile Company, founded by Herb Haughton, apparently towards the end of 1946. Herb and his bride, A. A. Burnand's step-daughter,

DEMARAIS COLLECTION - SAN DIEGO HISTORICAL SOCIETY RESEARCH ARCHIVES

Herb Haughton's original Borrego Springs store building, 1947

Charlotte Kuhrts, had spent their honeymoon at the Desert Lodge in 1939 and came back to live in the valley in 1945. They started their store in a trailer along Palm Canyon Drive and later moved to a tin building near where Lindberg's Borrego Pharmacy was later built on the south side of Palm Canyon Drive. Haughton also ran the local trucking business, hauling in merchandise for his store along with supplies for others.

BORREGO SUN

Woods' market on Christmas Circle in the 1950s.

Herb Haughton's sister-in-law, Bev Kuhrts, recalls: "...[he] would go to town once a week and bring back fresh groceries, and they had a funny little shack right at the west end of where Jilberto's is now. It just sat in the dirt, I don't think it was piped for anything, it was just like a big twelve-by-twelve shack where he would house all these fresh things. I remember the first day he brought ice cream to Borrego. He brought it in his truck...and everyone crowded around and they all had ice cream. It was like a celebration."[55]

DEMARAIS COLLECTION - SAN DIEGO HISTORICAL SOCIETY RESEARCH ARCHIVES

Bud's Cafe in its original Quonset hut, 1948.

In the spring of 1949 the Borrego Business Building on Christmas Circle opened, the first commercial building on the circle. The Haughtons moved in and ran the store until the summer of 1950, when they sold out to Julian grocers Hugh and Carol Woods. The Woodses renamed the store Woods Complete Food Market. At first they spent most of their time at their Julian store, hiring Wes Penrod as the first of several local managers. But as the years went by, they turned more and more of their attention to Borrego Springs.

Hugh Woods served two terms as chamber of commerce president in 1952 and '53, and endeared himself to local children by celebrating his birthday each year, beginning with his 48th in 1954, with a come-one, come-all party at the market. Woods was also noted as the valley's leading sports car enthusiast. A racing accident in 1957 cost him a leg, but he remained an active part of the community for the next twenty years, finally selling the market to Richard and Virginia Tynan in 1977. Borrego Valley Foods, as the Tynans renamed it, continues to operate today in the same location.

The first eating house in town (one hesitates to call it a restaurant), was Bud's Cafe, which was already a going concern when the tract went on sale in March of 1947. It was the first of Bud Kuhrts' many Borrego enterprises. "Buddy started the Quonset huts when he got out of the Navy," his widow, Bev, says. "It was called Bud's Cafe.

AUTHOR'S COLLECTION

The artist's rendering for the Borrego Pharmacy building, 1950.

He bought three Quonset huts; one in the front used for a restaurant, one on the side was a pool room, and then the third one was to house the gas and electric men and the road crews that were starting Borrego and bringing electricity. I remember him quoting, 'seven dollars a day for board and room.' So that went on for several years and then he leased the restaurant Quonset hut out to a wonderful mother and three daughters, and if you don't think they were popular, because they knew how to make pie! So everyone would stop at Bud's Cafe, the Quonset hut, for fresh pie."[56] One of Kuhrts' old Quonset huts still serves as a restaurant today.

The first service station in Borrego Springs was a Union Oil station on the northwest side of Christmas Circle, co-owned by Jack Benson and movie stuntman King Mojave, which opened in 1948. King Mojave ran the station for a time, then it was purchased by Paul Middlesworth. Norris Bakko seems to have owned the station for a while around 1953-54, then Middlesworth took over again. While he ran the service station his wife, Betty, ran Borrego Clothiers downtown. Eventually the Union station was moved to the corner of Palm Canyon Drive and Country Club Road.

Norris Bakko (1906-1994) had come to Borrego Springs in the spring of 1948 to work on the construction of the original Hoberg's Desert Resort. In 1949 he built a Chevron station across from the Desert Lodge. Bakko leased out his Chevron station in 1955 and went into the real estate business. He was one of the valley's most active boosters until his death. He also served as Honorary Mayor in 1987 and organized the annual Founders Day celebrations.

In April, 1950, L. W. and Marguerite Lindberg, known to all as Lindy and Peggy, opened Borrego's first drug store in the building which still stands at 649 Palm Canyon Drive. Their Borrego Rexall Pharmacy also featured a soda fountain and grill. Lindy had been selling real estate in San Diego when he was attracted to the valley by visits to Hoberg's Desert Resort. Peggy (1917-1994) was the pharmacist, a profession she learned from her father.

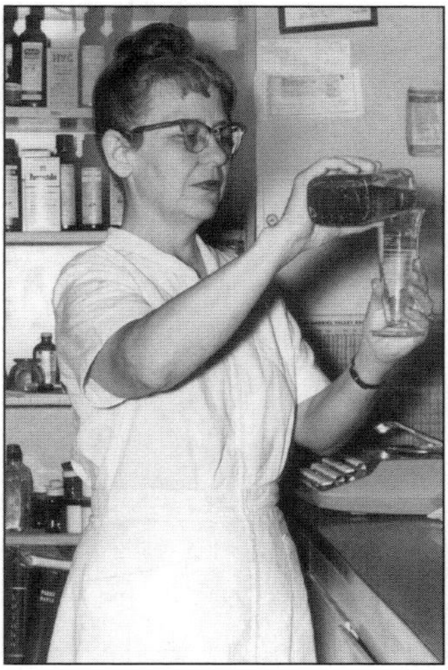
BORREGO SUN

Peggy Lindberg at work in the pharmacy, 1966.

The Lindbergs ran the pharmacy until 1961, when they sold out. Peggy continued to serve as pharmacist for the new owners until her retirement in 1972. Lindy opened a new store, the Village Trading Post, which he closed the same year his wife retired. They died just a few months apart in 1994.

Borrego's first resident physician was Dr. E. D. Neville, who came to the valley from Bellflower in 1950. His wife, Louise, was a registered nurse who assisted him in his practice. A World War II veteran, Dr. Neville had owned property in the valley since 1948. His first office was in the Lindberg Pharmacy building, but in 1952 Dave Mercer completed a new medical office building on the circle and Dr. Neville moved in. Dr. Neville served the community for six years, until 1956. His departure left the valley without a resident physician for several years.

The chamber of commerce placed ads in the *Journal of the American Medical Association*, hoping to lure a new practitioner to town.[57] Finally, in 1961, Dr. Marshall Stamper moved to Borrego from Pacific Beach and maintained his practice here until 1965.

At different times during the 1950s, various San Diego County dentists devoted a few days each month to keep a dental office open next door to Dr. Neville in the medical building. Dr. William Rice was the first, beginning in 1953. In 1954 Dr. Vinton Merrill was keeping the office open two days a week. In 1960, Dr. Dale Burke of La Mesa decided to reopen the office one week each month.

As Borrego Springs grew, other smaller businesses began to appear. Margaret Jackson opened the Marg-A-Reta Hand Crafts Shop in 1950, and ran it into the 1960s. In 1961 she moved into the new El Patio Shopping Center. The Nolan Appliance shop opened in 1951. Mr. and Mrs. Joe Kulas had both the Borrego Launderette and Borrego Clothiers in the early 1950s. They left the valley in 1953. The Circle S Liquor Store opened around 1952 and went through a string of owners before finally closing in 1959. What is now Carlee's Restaurant on the west side of Christmas Circle opened as La Placita in April, 1956. Actor Lon Chaney, Jr.'s, son, Ron Chaney, bought the place in 1963 and ran it for several years.

Other service businesses also began to appear. Julian architect Dick Zerbe established a branch office in Borrego in 1951. Lou Hahne (1901-1992) was the leading local auto mechanic in the early '50s. In 1954 he built a service station at the corner of Palm Canyon Drive and DiGiorgio Road, now the Ed Perry Tire Company, which he ran until 1976.

One thing that Borrego lacked for many years was a bank. Petitions to establish a local bank were circulated in 1957, but nothing ever came of it. Instead, local boosters began looking for an existing bank to open a Borrego branch. Both Imperial Savings and Loan of El Centro and San Diego Federal Savings looked into the matter, but decided against it. San Diego Federal Savings did agree to offer local real estate loans, and William Black, one of A. A. Burnand's later partners, organized the First Borrego Finance Company to handle local applications. Borrego Finance opened its doors in December, 1959, with Jack Russell as manager.

Borrego finally gained a bank in 1963 when the First National Bank of San Diego opened a branch in the valley. The valley's only local bank, Borrego Springs Bank, opened in 1982.

ADJOINING TRACTS

Modern Borrego Springs was the biggest, but not the only, tract laid out in the valley in the 1940s and '50s. In the late 1940s, Noel Crickmer laid out what he called the Rancho Borrego tract, adjoining the Desert Lodge to the south and east. It was included in the sale of the Lodge to the Kuhrtses in 1947, and in November, 1950, the *Borrego Sun* reported the first five houses were under construction on the tract.

In 1947 Ed Fletcher, Jr., the son of one of San Diego County's most prominent developers, laid out the Borrego Air Ranch in the southeast part of the valley, in the area the old homesteaders had dubbed Sleepy Hollow. This unusual subdivision includes a landing strip and individual hangers for its flying owners. Fletcher, who had learned to fly in the old Army Air Corps during World War I, was one of many Southern California pilots who discovered the Borrego Valley by air in the 1940s and '50s. Originally the ranch was just a weekend hideaway for Fletcher and a few of his friends, who were said to have acquired the property "from an army doctor who couldn't stand the desert solitude any longer."[58]

BORREGO SUN

Tom Davis, longtime manager of the Ensign Ranch, watches the growth of the Borrego Springs Park development on the ranch in the early 1960s.

The Deep Well Trail Number One subdivision south of the Desert Lodge was placed on the market in 1955 by Bud Kuhrts and Jack Benson, operating as the Golden Sands Corporation. In 1959 they opened Deep Well Number Two, along the west side of Borrego Valley Road, with 202 small residential lots.

Kuhrts and Benson, this time as the Sunny Borrego Corporation, were also responsible for the two Ocotillo Heights subdivisions on the south end of the original Borrego Springs tract, east of Borrego Springs Road. The 235 lots there went on sale in 1959.

Morgan Manor...was originally laid out by actor Frank Morgan, who played the wizard in *The Wizard of Oz.*

Morgan Manor, situated between the Borrego Springs tract and the De Anza Country Club along Lazy S Drive, was originally laid out by actor Frank Morgan, who played the wizard in *The Wizard of Oz*. He bought the property back in the late 1930s, but he died in the summer of 1949 before any lots were sold. The tract was tied up in his estate until 1960, when the Borrego Valley Associates were finally able to place the forty-seven half-acre lots on the market.

BORREGO ELEMENTARY SCHOOL

The old one-room Borego School continued to serve the valley until the end of the 1940s. In 1948, Borrego Springs voters approved a $34,000 bond act to replace the old school. The original plan was to build three new classrooms, but as it turned out, the money would pay for only two, so the old building would have to make do for a few more years. The new building was completed at the end of 1949. Two new classrooms meant two new teachers for Borrego Elementary. Joining Dolores O'Connor, who had taught in the valley since 1947, were Lona Bishop and Beverly Jacobs, soon to be Mrs. Perry Burnand. Bishop served as principal and taught first

BORREGO SUN

The Borrego Springs Elementary School campus from the air, 1967.

and second grades; O'Connor taught third, fourth and fifth grades; and Jacobs taught sixth, seventh and eighth grades.

With the completion of the modern classrooms, the Kiwanis Club began the improvement of the school grounds. Between 1950 and 1952, lawns and sidewalks were laid out, date palms and mulberry trees were planted, and a flagpole was erected.

Enrollment at the beginning of 1950 was sixty students, and there were ten graduates in June, 1951. Though enrollment had climbed over one hundred by 1957, the number of eighth grade graduates remained fairly constant through the 1950s, dropping as low as eight in 1953 and '55, and climbing to a high of thirteen in 1959.

Two more modern classrooms were added in 1951, and the old school building was finally retired. For a while it served as the custodian's residence, but in 1958 it was sold to Lou Hahne, who moved it to his service station. There it housed an auto parts store for many years, and then stood empty for a time before, sadly, being destroyed in an arson fire in 1994.

Lona Bishop served as principal until 1953, followed by Anna Miller. From 1954-58 Justine Mathis was principal and also taught grades seven and eight. In 1958 the school was finally large enough to require a full-time principal, and Jack Carter was hired. At the same time, Virginia DeMarais, who had been working in the office for several years, was hired full-time as school secretary.

The elementary school district had a three-member Board of Trustees, elected by the community. Wes Harris served for most of the 1950s, and when he retired in 1958, Norman Gilbert was elected to his old seat. Harris returned to the board briefly in 1961, but resigned in 1962. Dr. E. D. Neville served on the board almost the entire time he was in the valley. He was appointed in 1951 and resigned when he moved away in 1956. Rancher George Shintaku served from 1951-55.

One of the first projects of the new district was the construction of Borrego Springs High School, which opened in 1965. Never again would valley students have to go up the mountain to Julian to earn a high school diploma.

In 1959 Anza-Borrego Desert State Park ranger John McGinnis announced his candidacy for the School Board, then discovered, too late to keep his name off the ballot, that he would soon be transferred to another park. So McGinnis organized a write-in campaign for Victor Blurton who was elected in his place. Blurton was later re-elected in his own right and was the only member of the old elementary school district board to be elected to the new five-member unified school district Board of Trustees in 1963.

A ninety-thousand-dollar auditorium was built for the elementary school in 1957, and in 1959 three new primary classrooms were built, including Borrego's first kindergarten. The kindergarten teacher in 1960-61 was a familiar face to old timers; Emalyn Holland was back in Borrego after an absence of nearly twenty years, to finish up her long teaching career.

The old Borrego Elementary School District (the second "r" having been officially added in 1950), was replaced in 1963 by the Borrego Unified School District. One of the first projects of the new district was the construction of Borrego Springs High School, which opened in 1965. Never again would valley students have to go up the mountain to Julian to earn a high school diploma.

CHURCHES

In 1948, Father Francis Lobell, a Catholic priest from Idaho, came to Julian seeking a milder climate. During the winter of 1948-49 he divided his time between Julian and Borrego Springs and began offering Mass at Hoberg's Desert Resort. In the spring of 1949 the Bishop of San Diego officially appointed him resident priest at Julian.

The original plan for Borrego Springs had called for a "municipal center" at the foot of the hills at the top of T Anchor Drive. This soon became the church area, and in 1949, under the direction of Norris Bakko, a large cross was erected on the hill above. Father Lobell was the first to take advantage of this opportunity, and by the beginning of 1949 had secured a site for what was being called the De Anza Catholic Mission. Services, however, continued to be held at Hoberg's until 1954.

Fund-raising for a church began in 1952, and by the summer of 1953 construction was underway. But Father Lobell would not live to see the church completed. He died in the fall of 1953, and Father

BORREGO SUN

Local residents placed a cross on the ridge above the future "church row" during Easter, 1949.

William Cooney was sent from Beaumont to serve both St. Elizabeth's in Julian, which was built under Father Lobell's direction in 1950, and the De Anza mission in Borrego.

The De Anza name did not survive. On April 25, 1954, Borrego Springs' first church was dedicated as St. Richard's Catholic Church. Father Cooney continued as pastor until July of that year, when Father Dennis Magnum was sent to Borrego. Father Magnum served until the end of 1959, when he was transferred to Vista.

His replacement, Father Charles Young, served less than one year. It was during his tenure, in April, 1960, that a fire of unknown origin destroyed the altar area inside St. Richard's. Fortunately the rest of the building was undamaged, and services continued as repairs were made. In the summer of 1960, Father Young was transferred to Barstow, and Father Thomas Byrnes became pastor of St. Richard's. The congregation is still active today, having been made a full parish in 1968.

In 1947-48, Rev. R. S. Wallis of the Julian Baptist Church was conducting Sunday School classes in Borrego. The first Protestant church in the valley was the Borrego Springs Community Church, which was already holding regular services by the beginning of 1949. In the first issue of the *Borrego Sun*, pastor Charles Olson described it as the "Bor(r)ego Community Church." Services were then being held in "the little white schoolhouse." Soon after, the church moved into the new market building on Christmas Circle, where services were held until 1955.

The congregation was formally organized in 1950, with *Sun* editor Paul Strand as the chairman of the Board of Trustees. Rev. T. A. Homme served as pastor that year, followed by a Rev. Wickwire in 1951. During his tenure the church was renamed the Borrego United Church.

Rev. Wickwire left near the end of 1951, and Rev. J. S. Fox came to serve as interim pastor. He secured a promise of a church site from the Land and Development Company and in December, 1951, announced plans for a building campaign. The church went through a string of interim pastors in 1952, including Dr. William Jones, who died that July, Rev. Maynard and Dr. Alfred Hughes, a prominent old Southern California Methodist minister.

Though originally planned as a "non-denominational Protestant church" with the slogan, "Of the Community, by the Community, for the Community," in 1952 the congregation chose to affiliate with the Methodist Church. The congregation had approached the San Diego Council of Churches some time back looking for support, and the Methodists seemed most willing to provide it. On December 1, 1952, the new Borrego Springs Methodist Church received its first regularly appointed pastor from the Southern California-Arizona Conference, Rev. J. Wilbur Hadley, who had been serving as the Associate Pastor of the Central Methodist Church in Phoenix, Arizona.

A parsonage was built for Rev. Hadley in 1953, and in 1954 a sanctuary was designed and serious fund-raising began. Austen Cargill provided much of the funding for the sanctuary. Ground-breaking was held in the spring of 1955, and the first services in the new building were held October 9 that same year under Rev. Hadley's successor, Rev. Robert Stanley. This is the sanctuary still used by the Borrego Springs Community United Methodist Church today.

BORREGO SUN

Services continue in St. Richard's Catholic Church after a fire which destroyed the altar area in April, 1960.

The Methodist Church has always worked on an appointment system, with the local Bishop and his advisors determining where each pastor will serve each year. Pastors are usually moved every few years; thus Rev. Stanley was followed by Rev. Richard Avery in 1958, who was followed by Rev. Samuel Spear in 1960.

BORREGO SUN

The Reverend Richard Avery arrives as the new pastor of the Borrego Springs Community Methodist Church, 1958.

Several other denominations held services with visiting pastors from time to time, but the only other Borrego congregation organized during the 1950s was the Seventh Day Adventists, who began meeting in the home of Mr. and Mrs. Ward Hutton in 1955, under the leadership of Elder Hollis Anderson. Ward Hutton (1912-1987), a devout Adventist, brought his family to the valley in 1947 and owned and operated the Borrego Dump Truck Service from 1952-75. Services continued in his home for eleven years, until the congregation arranged to begin using the Methodist Church for their Saturday morning services.

BORREGO SPRINGS POST OFFICE

The Borrego Valley had been without a post office since the old Borego Post Office had been closed in 1940. For the next nine years Borrego received its mail via the Borego Star Route, with homesteader Al Mathes often doing the driving. (Star routes were an old system of contract mail delivery). Finally, in 1949, after a year of bureaucratic red tape, the application was approved for a new Borrego Springs Post Office. Gertrude Steffen, a clerk in Haughton's

Borrego Mercantile, was sworn in as postmaster, and the office officially opened in the store building on May 16, 1949.

The original delivery service was just three days a week, with Al Mathes still hauling the mail down from Julian. In 1952 delivery was extended to Ocotillo Wells and Agua Caliente Hot Springs, with George Smith driving the mail. Official post office boxes became available at the end of 1949. *Borrego Sun* founder Paul Strand seems to have been the first to hold P. O. Box 1. Later, Wes and Virginia Harris had Box 1. DiGiorgio's Borrego Farms had Box A, and A. A. Burnand had Box B, those being the large, commercial-size boxes.

Virginia Harris (1910-1979) took over as postmaster in 1950 and served for more than a quarter of a century. Sometime in the early '50s the post office moved into the pharmacy building. Then in 1961 Harrison Baker, one of Burnand's original partners, built a new post office building for Borrego at the south end of the Plaza Shopping Center, which served until the present post office was built in 1986.

THE *BORREGO SUN*

Real estate sales and newspapers have always gone hand-in-hand in Southern California, and Borrego Springs was only a few months old when it entered the journalism game. The first Borrego Springs publication was *Borrego Desert Life*, a promotional magazine founded in 1948, presumably with the backing of A. A. Burnand and his partners. It was printed in Santa Monica and seems to have survived for only two issues.

May, 1949, saw the birth of the *Borrego Sun*. Paul Strand (1907-1994), a Glendale real estate agent, had become interested in the development of Borrego Springs and decided that what the new desert community needed was a newspaper. Although he had only limited newspaper experience, Strand plunged right in as editor, publisher and everything else. "I tracked down all the news, took pictures, plus I did all the ad sales, layout and artwork," he recalled years later.[59] The four-page monthly was printed in Los Angeles and available to subscribers at a cost of one dollar per year. The initial circulation was about one hundred.

BORREGO SUN

James Copley presents Virginia DeMarais with a copy of the first issue of the Borrego Sun *as the paper celebrated its twentieth anniversary in 1969.*

Despite Strand's lack of experience and the hardships of starting a newspaper in a new, isolated desert community, the early issues of the *Borrego Sun* aren't half bad. Printed on quality white paper, the original masthead tip-toed around the then-current controversy over the correct spelling of "Borrego" by spelling it correctly with two "r"s, but leaving the second "r" shaded out to cater to the old "one r" crowd. The contents of the first issue are typical of the *Sun*'s coverage during the years to come: road work, wildflowers, local businesses, and society notes from the local resorts. Later, more news on local agriculture and organizations would be added.

In 1951, Strand decided to leave the desert heat and return to his home in Glendale, so he sold the *Sun* to the Borrego Springs Company. At the time, the circulation was around two hundred, but the Borrego Springs Company soon began using the paper as a promotional tool, printing thousands of copies that they distributed free throughout Southern California. By the end of 1952 the company was claiming ten thousand readers for each issue.

BORREGO SUN

Vol. 1 BORREGO VALLEY, APRIL, 1949 10c per copy No. 2

Turnage Hotel

The new Turnage Hotel is to be erected shortly. The building contract for this hotel has been given to Golden Construction Company of San Diego. We understand the area will include a large clubhouse, swimming pool, and forty-eight cottage units. The cost of this new venture is estimated at $250,000. Another milestone in the progress of Borrego Valley!

Church Social

An informal social gathering of the children and young people of the Borrego Community church is

Borrego Wild Flowers Attract Thousands

The beautiful display of wild flowers this year is considered to be the greatest in a decade. During a recent week-end it has been estimated by highway authorities to have attracted nearly 16,000 automobiles. Cars were crawling bumper to bumper throughout Borrego valley. Some observers claimed the steady stream of cars was a solid mass reaching as far as Ramona. What a sight this would have been for Capt De Anza and his party of trail blazers!

Men, women, and children

Soil Conservation Proposed

Mr. A. N. Chammess, vice-president of the State Soil

AUTHOR'S COLLECTION

The second issue of the Borrego Sun, *showing the original masthead.*

During the years the Borrego Springs Company owned the *Sun*, the paper went through a rapid succession of editors, including Ed Phillips, Jim Downs, Bill DeMarais, Dick Wear, and Sandy Bothman. It was during DeMarais' tenure that his wife, Virginia, began her association with the paper, which would survive through all the changes in editors and owners for the next forty-two years.

At the beginning of 1954, Borrego Valley Associates (Bud Kuhrts and Jack Benson) took over the paper, just as they had taken over many of the old functions of the Borrego Springs Company. The Associates held the paper for barely three months before turning it over to a new owner who would have much to do with the valley's future, Jim Copley, the president of The Copley Press. Included in the deal was the Associates' new editor, Polly Baker. Copley then appointed Dick Johnson of his flagship publication, *The San Diego Union*, as general manager.[60]

With the new owner, the *Sun* finally got a new masthead, the original shaded-r artwork being replaced by the current script design. A year later, the *Sun*, now printed at Copley's La Jolla plant, opened its first local office, with chamber of commerce secretary Paula Sullivan handling ad sales. Copley also moved his annual "Copley Conferences" to Borrego Springs, beginning with the forty-sixth annual conference in 1955, held in the new Kiva Room at the Desert Lodge. The conferences, still held in Borrego, bring together all of Copley's executive staff from across the nation for workshops and discussions and to hear prominent guest speakers.

In 1959, Copley announced plans to build a separate office building for the *Sun* along Christmas Circle. By then, circulation had risen to over eighteen hundred paid subscribers. When completed in 1960, the building was also home to the new First Borrego Finance Company. Today the *Sun* occupies the entire building. It is still owned by The Copley Press and has been published biweekly since 1965.

COMMUNITY ORGANIZATIONS

The Borrego Springs Community Association has always been "the nearest thing this unincorporated community has in the way of a local governing organization."[61] The Community Association was formed in 1949 by A. A. Burnand and his partners and reflects their vision of the future of Borrego Springs. According to the *Sun*, "[Burnand's] stepson, George Kuhrts III, said that...he had...ideas of developing an ideal desert community. He wanted to protect it from becoming a hodge-podge of desert "shacks" and make it an attractive, affordable place for people to live.

"It was this thought that started an association to control building and growth in Borrego Springs, Kuhrts said, and was the foundation for the deed restrictions now a part of the Community Association."[62]

In many ways, the Borrego Springs Community Association was similar to a modern homeowners' association, responsible for the enforcement of deed restrictions established by the original developers; for example, a requirement that homebuilders could not remove more than ten percent of the native growth around their homes. In 1949, this was still a novel idea. The Community Association also was given charge of various community amenities, from the care of Christmas Circle to trash collection.

The first president of the Community Association was Lawrence Barker. The second was Burnand partner Harrison Baker. Later presidents include Margaret Jackson (1958) and Fred Woods (1960). All local property owners were voting members of the association.

Another part of A. A. Burnand's vision for his recreational desert community was the Borrego Springs Desert Club, which opened in February, 1950. This was in effect Borrego Springs' first country club, and all purchasers of the larger estate lots in the tract

AUTHOR'S COLLECTION

The Borrego Springs Desert Club was the valley's first country club; it opened in 1950.

were given memberships. The Desert Club featured a clubhouse, a swimming pool and the beginnings of a golf course. Hollywood stuntman and Borrego service station manager King Mojave was the first manager, followed in 1951 by Mr. and Mrs. Ray Johnson.

The Borrego Springs Land and Development Company began construction on the Desert Club in September, 1949, and deeded the property over to the members in 1952. During the 1950s the board of directors was headed by some prominent Borrego names, including Rupert Hauser, Bud Kuhrts, Jack Benson and Austen Cargill.

Along with Hoberg's, the Desert Club hosted many community events in the early 1950s. "Guest Chef Night" proved especially popular, with local residents each taking turns to cook for the members. "I remember I did Salisbury steaks one night," Sam Fortiner recalls, "and I think I cooked 180-some of them."[63] But after the De Anza Country Club opened in 1957, the focus shifted to the newer, larger facility. Burnand and his partners had originally set aside about a hundred acres surrounding the Desert Club with an eye to future development, but that land was sold off in 1964. The final three acres, including the clubhouse and pool, were finally sold to Robert and Sophia Schepe in 1968, who opened the Galeria de Anza-Borrego in the old building.

The Borrego Springs Chamber of Commerce was founded in 1948 and held its first meeting at Hoberg's Desert Resort that fall. The chamber was going strong in 1950, but by 1954 was at a low ebb. That fall, a new group of community leaders led by Jack Marovich formed the Borrego Business Boosters, to serve as something of a tourist bureau for the valley. In 1955, when the chamber was revitalized, the boosters added their support and became a chamber committee. Paula Sullivan was hired as chamber manager and served until 1958.

The first president of the chamber seems to have been Phil Ellis of Hoberg's Desert Resort. He was followed in 1949 by Bill DeMarais; there were already 113 members by then. Next came Jack Benson (1950), "Lindy" Lindberg (1951), Hugh Woods (1952-53), Wick Hauser (1954), Wes Harris (1955-56), Dave Mercer (1957),

AUTHOR'S COLLECTION

The charter members of the Borrego Springs Kiwanis Club posing soon after their midnight organizational meeting on January 1, 1950. Shown, left to right, are: (front row) Les Furnas, D. Smith, Mark Steffen, King Mojave, K. O. Burt, Win Ward, Bill DeMarais, and Frank Harmon; (middle row) Wes Harris, Robert Ransom, Roy Gentel, A. A. Burnand, Jr., Ed Jackson, Jack Shinn, Don Castle, B. Beck, Ed Bishop, Al Martinez, Herb Haughton, and Paul Ensign; (back row) Dwight Raver, Jack Benson, Frank Hermance, Lon Chaney, Jr., Barney White, Bob Beck, Don Chaney, and Paul Strand.

the return of Wes Harris (1958), and Stu Haseltine rounding out the decade in 1959. Patrick Nolan served as president in 1960 and was then hired as chamber manager in 1961, when actor Gale Gordon was serving as president.

The Junior Chamber of Commerce, "Jaycees," was organized in February, 1959, with twenty-five charter members, who elected John Horvat as president. In 1960 the Jaycees backed the creation of a "Teenagers Club" for the valley to sponsor dances and social activities for local teens. Frank Martinez was the teen club's first president.

The first service club in the valley was the Borrego Springs Kiwanis Club, which held its organizational meeting at Hoberg's just a few minutes after midnight on New Year's Day, 1950, so that it could be the first new Kiwanis Club in the nation for 1950. There were twenty-eight charter members. Bob Beck was the first president, but soon had to step down due to business pressures. Jack Shinn filled out the rest of his term, with Ed Jackson following as president for 1951.

One of the Kiwanis Club's first community contributions was the sponsorship of a Boy Scout troop, which was organized early in 1950, with fourteen boys and Bob Gentel as Scoutmaster, followed by Ward Hutton. The troop lapsed sometime in 1951, but was reorganized at the start of 1952 as Troop 111 (later changed to 661), with Fred Gardner as Scoutmaster. In the late 1950s the troop again faltered, but was revived in 1960 under Scoutmaster Lee Hickey. Through all its ups and downs, the Kiwanis Club remained the sponsor.

BORREGO SUN

Santa Claus (Bill Burford) passed out gifts in Christmas Circle to all of Borrego's children, 1958.

The first Girl Scout group in the valley was Troop 411, organized in October, 1950, with twelve girls and Mrs. R. B. Bell as troop leader. In 1953, a Brownie troop was added for younger girls.

In 1953, under president "Lindy" Lindberg, the club announced plans for a valley youth activity center on the grounds of the elementary school. Construction began that year, and the center was dedicated in June, 1954. The Kiwanis Club remained active through the end of the 1950s, but lapsed in the mid-1960s. The Lions Club eventually took over the youth center, and in 1972 the facilities were deeded over to the nonprofit Borrego Springs Youth Center.

Like so many other local groups, the Borrego Springs Post of the American Legion held its organizational meeting at Hoberg's Desert Resort. The post was officially chartered in the spring of 1950, with twenty-three charter members. Ben Sutton was the first post com-

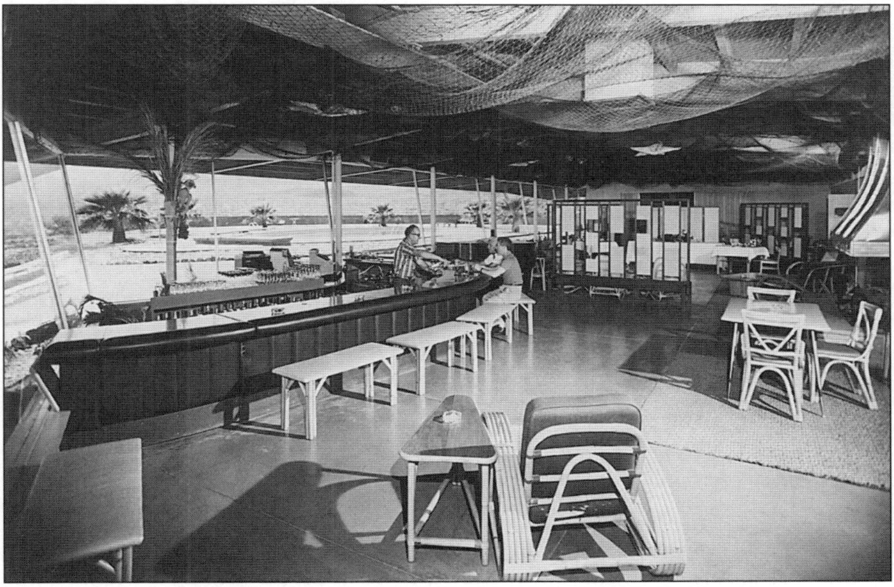

DEMARAIS COLLECTION - SAN DIEGO HISTORICAL SOCIETY RESEARCH ARCHIVES

Inside the Desert Club, 1960.

mander, with Jack Benson as first vice president and Al Mathes serving as chaplain.

The post's first goal was to build a Legion Hall in the valley. They secured a site on T Anchor near the church area, broke ground in 1952, and received approval from the county for their plans in 1953, but that was as far as the project ever went.

The Legionnaires continued to meet for several more years, but numbers finally dwindled to the point that the Borrego Springs Post was deactivated, and the remaining members reorganized as a chapter of the Ramona Post. The present Borrego Springs American Legion Post was not chartered until some years later.

Local Masons formed a Square & Compass Club in 1950, which survived into the mid-1960s. One of their traditional activities was an annual children's Christmas party in Christmas Circle (where else?). Club members and their wives bought gifts for every child in the valley. "We...had a wrapping party at our motel and individually tagged each gift," Virginia DeMarais recalled. "We bought the boys and girls gifts for each age group. The men had the most fun assembling the toys, especially the popular red wagons."[64] Later the Borrego Springs Mothers' Club took over the party until the number of children in town just grew too large.

> **"We bought the boys and girls gifts for each age group. The men had the most fun assembling the toys, especially the popular red wagons."**
>
> ***Virginia DeMarais***

Borrego has supported several community Little Theater groups over the years. The first was organized in 1949 by Borrego Elementary School teacher Dolores O'Connor. Lon Chaney, Jr., directed some of their first plays. A new theater group, the De Anza Players, was organized in 1954. Former radio actress and longtime *Borrego Sun* reporter Polly Baker served as their director until 1961.

For those with simpler tastes, Borrego Springs had a homemade drive-in theater in the early 1950s. It was located just west of the Borrego Pharmacy. Bev Kuhrts recalls: "They took bulldozers and reamed up the ground in humps so people could park facing up toward the screen, and they had a little restroom under this building and the screen on top of it, and all the kids came for a big-time Saturday night out. It was fantastic."[65]

JUDICIAL MATTERS

The old Borego Township Justice Court continued to serve the valley into the early years of Borrego Springs. Al Mathes was serving as justice of the peace in the late 1940s. The job was not all that taxing. According to Virginia DeMarais, he heard only three cases in 1949-50, but his case load doubled to six in 1950-51.

At the end of 1951, L. W. "Lindy" Lindberg was appointed Borrego's new justice of the peace and held court, when he had to, in the drug store. Early in 1952 he was called upon to perform his first wedding, when *Borrego Sun* editor Jim Downs married Mary Caturegli at Hoberg's. "I think the Judge was more nervous than the groom," Virginia DeMarais later recalled.[66]

Judge Lindberg served until 1953, when he resigned. He was followed by George Gutteridge, but when he resigned in May, 1954, the post was left vacant and the justice court allowed to lapse. The Board of Supervisors ignored local requests to reestablish a Borrego Court, in 1958 and again in 1965. At first, local cases had to travel clear to the court in Jacumba, but later Borrego Springs was placed under the Ramona Judicial Court.

Along with the justice court, the Borego Township also had its own part-time deputy sheriff. Eddie DuVall continued to fill that role for several years after Borrego Springs began. It was not until 1957 that the valley got its first full-time, resident deputy sheriff, Jim Scott, who served until 1961.

BORREGO SPRINGS BRANCH LIBRARY

The Borrego Springs Branch of the San Diego County Free Public Library opened on May 10, 1949, at Bill and Virginia DeMarais' Hacienda Borrego motel. Virginia recalled: "The San Diego County Library was introduced in Borrego in May, 1949, established in our motel office. Nothing like having a library in your front room. We always had something to read. There were two tall shelves of books. We received $3.39 per month to run this tiny library, keeping it for a couple of years before it was moved over to a business in the town site. Our space was too limited for the library to expand."[67]

The county paid the rent, and Virginia served as librarian until the library was moved into Margaret Jackson's Marg-A-Reta shop in 1951. Jackson then served as librarian until the books were moved to a third location, in Lee's Laundromat in the Borrego Pharmacy Building. In 1970, the library was moved to The Plaza, which it occupied until October, 2000, when it was moved to its current location in The Mall.

BORREGO SPRINGS AIRPORT

One way the Borrego Valley has worked to overcome its natural isolation is through air travel. A number of Borrego's early boosters and residents often flew in and out of the valley, including the Hobergs, Herb Haughton, Robert Ransom, Al Burnand III, Ed Fletcher, Jr., and Sam Fortiner. Fortiner remembers flying over to Ocotillo Wells in the '40s, when that was the closest telephone to the valley. "I used to fly over to Hoberg's to get a haircut," he adds, "it was quicker by far to fly over there than to drive over there."[68]

These pioneer pilots tended to land where they pleased, sometimes even on Palm Canyon Drive. Hoberg's resort and the Ensign Ranch both had their own private air strips. A. A. Burnand, Jr., took the lead in the construction of a community air strip, beginning in 1946, and then donated the site to San Diego County. More work was done in 1949, and the $40,000 Borrego Springs Airport was officially dedicated on the first of May of that year. The *Borrego Sun* called it, "the biggest thing that has happened for the valley since the completion of the Hoberg Hotel."

The county leased the airport to a succession of managers during the 1950s, including Herb Haughton, Arden Connick, Fred Brockbeck, "Red" Hathaway and Charles Miller. Miller, a retired Air Force Lieutenant Colonel, tried offering regular passenger flights to Brawley and San Diego in 1957, but that service left with him at the end of the year. Ed Mitrani followed as manager and, finally, in 1959, Ben Audette, who had the Molino Verde Motel across the street, took over.

Regular passenger service to and from Borrego Springs finally began in 1969. As with many other projects, A. A. Burnand took the lead in gathering the investors to form Borrego Springs Airline. DiGiorgio bought out the company in 1974, and it was renamed Sun Aire. Skywest Airlines bought them out in 1984. One of the conditions of the sale was that they continue to serve Borrego Springs for the next five years. They did that, but no more, and Borrego Springs has been without regular commercial passenger service since 1989.

BORREGO SUN

Thousands of people gathered at the Borrego Springs Airport in April, 1961, for a two-day "Aero-Rama" flying show. Over five hundred planes participated.

DE ANZA COUNTRY CLUB

One look at Palm Springs, even in the 1940s, showed the developers of Borrego Springs that desert resorts were expected to have a golf course. A. A. Burnand had tried to get a course going at the Desert Club in the late 1940s, and in 1953 a little "pitch and putt" course was laid out across the road from the Desert Lodge; but creating a modern, eighteen-hole course would take some time.

Plans finally began to come together in 1953, with the creation of the Borrego Valley Golf and Improvement Association. The *Sun* reported: "Spearheading the drive, which is hailed as one of the most important in Borrego history, are Adm. Ralph Wood, USN (ret.), Rupert W. Hauser, Dr. Eugene Neville, John J. Kovacevich, Robert DiGiorgio, A. A. Burnand, Jr., N. Jack Benson, George J. Kuhrts III, William Hoppe, and William T. Johnson.

"As organizers of the Borrego Valley Golf and Improvement Association, they have underwritten a $10,000 fund to meet preliminary expenses, and have secured pledges of an additional $90,000 from golf enthusiasts in Southern California."[69]

BORREGO SUN

Construction begins on the Fairways tract adjoining the De Anza Country Club golf course, 1958.

Led by president Bud Kuhrts and vice president Robert DiGiorgio, by 1954 the Association had selected a site and a name for their proposed development. The De Anza Country Club would be located on the old Riverall Ranch, on the northwest side of the valley. The ranch was at that time owned by A. A. Burnand. In addition to the country club, plans were also developed for a residential subdivision surrounding the golf course.

The Golf and Improvement Association was formed as a stock company to underwrite the construction costs. All stockholders then became members of the country club. Stock went on sale at the beginning of 1955 at one thousand dollars per share. It took more than a year to sell the first 150 of the three hundred shares issued, and several of the directors of the Association bought blocks of stock to put the project over the top.

Meanwhile, in September of 1955, construction began on the first nine holes and a clubhouse. A well was sunk, the golf course graded, grass planted, and, curiously, beach sand was imported from Pebble Beach for the sandtraps. On May 12, 1956, a public drawing was held to distribute the residential lots among the buyers. The first lots made available were staggered in a checkerboard pattern, to allow a little more elbow room at the start. The first name drawn was Mrs. Rupert Hauser, and by November Perry Burnand had finished the first home in the new tract.

The De Anza Country Club officially opened on January 5, 1957. Over one hundred members and guests watched club president Austen Cargill hit the first drive down the fairway. Johnny Dawson, a 1930s amateur star, was the first golfer, and the only one that day, to make the course's seventy-two par. Players went twice around the nine-hole course to make their eighteen. Manuel Rodriguez, a superintendent at Borrego Farms, made the first hole-in-one on February 19 on the 178-yard seventh hole.

For non-stockholders, the original membership cost was one hundred dollars, plus twenty-five dollars a month dues. A sixty-dollar annual membership was also available, with annual members then paying a three-dollar green fee on weekdays and five dollars

BORREGO SUN

Crowds gathered to watch the celebrity foursomes during the 1960 PGA Pro-Am tournament at the De Anza Country Club.

on weekends. Special rates were also available to local motels and resorts for memberships to be used by their guests.

Frank Morey was the first course pro, and Austen Cargill, the last surviving son of the founder of Cargill, Inc., the huge Minnesota grain wholesale firm, served as the original club president at De Anza until his sudden death in May, 1957. Later Jim Copley, and Pat Patterson of United Airlines, would serve as De Anza presidents. In 1958, work began on the club's second nine holes, which opened on February 7, 1959, giving De Anza a full 6,613-yard, eighteen-hole course.

> **"At that time, the great hope was that if enough really important people discovered Borrego it could be planned properly, not trashed like a lot of these other desert communities."**
>
> ***Bev Kuhrts***

The year 1959 also marked De Anza's first major tournament, the Ryder Cup Pro-Am, featuring such pros as Sam Snead, Art Wall, Jr., and Bob Rosburg. Snead shot a four-under 68.

The De Anza Country Club was seen as an important step in the development of Borrego Springs, and it was. Real estate sales blossomed for the first year or two after the club opened, but then things settled back to normal. "At that time," says Bev Kuhrts, "the great hope was that if enough really important people discovered Borrego it could be planned properly, not trashed like a lot of these other desert communities. But unfortunately, or fortunately, they didn't want anyone else to know about Borrego, because they loved it so much themselves that they never really got on the bandwagon...to bring new people, new blood, new wealth into Borrego."[70]

A DESERT DREAM

By 1960 Borrego Springs had more or less become what it is today. The development that has followed has largely been in the patterns laid down in the 1940s and '50s. The valley's isolation continues to hamper its growth, or as some would say, keeps it from getting too big. At more than fifty years of age, Borrego Springs has yet to see its first traffic light.

BORREGO SUN

A. A. Burnand, Jr., in later years.

A. A. Burnand, Jr., lived to see what Borrego Springs became. He died in 1981 at the age of eighty-five. Was he satisfied with how his dream had turned out? "I think more or less," says his only surviving son, A. A. Burnand III. "He probably hoped that maybe it had developed a little bigger, or a little faster, but I think he was pretty well satisfied. He certainly saw that it wasn't going to be another Palm Springs or anything like that, but he was satisfied with that, I would say. In other words, probably starting out his dreams were bigger than the way it turned out, but he took it that way."[71]

NOTES

1. *Borrego Sun*, July 11, 1985. Fred Woods was the son of longtime Borego booster Harry Woods.
2. *San Diego Union*, December 7, 1981.
3. Personal interview, October 22, 1998. In the mid-1950s, DiGiorgio had ten thousand acres at Delano and five thousand acres at Arvin, along with over two thousand acres in the Borrego Valley.
4. *Borrego Sun*, November, 1956.
5. *San Diego Union*, February 11, 1945.
6. To promote the construction of railroads during the nineteenth century, the federal government had promised the railroad companies a subsidy in land for every mile of track laid. It was deeded over as alternating sections, 640 acres, in a checkerboard pattern. When the Southern Pacific built its line through the Coachella Valley in the late 1870s, their land subsidy included many sections in upper Coyote Canyon, the Santa Rosa Mountains and even as far down as Borrego Valley.
7. Baker was born in Los Angeles in 1894 where his father had been one of the developers of the Cahuenga tract (now a part of Hollywood) in 1888. In 1905 the family moved to Pasadena. In 1921, after service in the Navy in World War I, Baker formed Davis-Baker and Company with Richard Davis, and was a successful real estate developer and tract builder for many years. He died in 1970.
8. *San Diego Union*, November 5, 1946.
9. Palm Springs *Desert Sun*, March 25, 1947.
10. Philip Curti noted, "The fact that the San Diego Gas and Electric Company was permitted to obtain such vital material as copper during wartime is evidence of the importance attached to the Borrego Valley's food potential by the United States government." *The Borrego Valley: The Birth of a Desert Community* (unpublished Master's Thesis, University of California, Los Angeles), 1955.
11. The Borrego Springs Water Company was regulated as a public utility. Two private water companies were also formed in the 1950s to serve other parts of the valley; the Rancho Borrego Mutual Water Company and the Golden Sands Mutual Water Company, which served the Deep Well subdivisions. In the early 1960s the Borrego Springs Community Service District was formed to provide, among other things, water service for the Club Circle development on the old Ensign Ranch.
12. Personal interview, May 22, 1999.
13. *Desert* magazine, November, 1946.

14. *Westways*, December, 1947.
15. "*Facts About Borrego Springs...*", promotional brochure [1947]. Virginia DeMarais Collection.
16. Personal interview, March 27, 1999.
17. In November, 1950, the *Sun* reported that the Borrego Springs Company was bringing in guests from Los Angeles on DC-3s, twenty-eight at a time, for "cocktails, luncheon and a tour of the valley."
18. *Borrego Sun*, November, 1950.
19. *Borrego Sun*, July 19, 1990.
20. Personal interview, March 27, 1999.
21. *Borrego Sun*, July, 1955.
22. *Borrego Sun*, January, 1955. Burnand's new partners also bought a half interest in the Borrego Springs Water Company.
23. Personal interview, March 27, 1999.
24. *Borrego Sun*, February 28, 1991.
25. Future DiGiorgio projects in the valley would include the Mall (1966), the RoadRunner Club (1968), and Rams Hill in the 1980s. The DiGiorgio Corporation finally sold the last of its local holdings in 1988.
26. *Borrego Sun*, November, 1953.
27. In June, 1948, there were 102 registered voters in what was still called the Borego Precinct. But according to the original records in Virginia DeMarais' files, only twenty people voted in the primary election that month. In 1960 there were over 275 registered voters in Borrego Springs.
28. Philip Curti, *The Borrego Valley: The Birth of a Desert Community*, 1955. Curti reports that about three-quarters of the lots in Borrego Springs had been sold by the end of 1954.
29. *Borrego Sun*, July 15, 1961. Of 2,845 subdivided lots in the valley, only three hundred had houses on them. Including outlying properties, there were a total of 436 homes in the valley in 1960, the article points out. Borrego's population was 1,140 in 1965, and 1,607 in 1968.
30. *Borrego Sun*, July 15, 1961. Curti, in his thesis, notes, "The valley's future is based on the triple factors of agricultural development, residential subdivision, and recreational attraction. Each is interdependent upon the others...".
31. *Borrego Sun*, November, 1951.
32. By 1959, grape acreage in the valley was down to just under nineteen hundred acres, with DiGiorgio still leading the list with twelve hundred acres and the rest divided between the Flying M, 260 acres; Jack Russell and the Halfred Ranch (Hal Seely and Fred Levy) with 110 acres each; the Freeman Company, 160 acres; and Bill Hoppe and Dr. Leon Campbell, with just forty acres each.

33. Curti, *The Borrego Valley* (1955). In 1953, he reports, Borrego growers shipped 19,501 crates of table grapes—with about two-thirds of that total coming from DiGiorgio.
34. Curti, *The Borrego Valley* (1955). Most of the tree crops cited were not yet producing.
35. Personal correspondence, March 27, 1999.
36. *Borrego Sun*, November, 1954.
37. Personal interview, March 27, 1999.
38. Personal correspondence, March 27, 1999.
39. Personal interview, May 22, 1999.
40. Personal interview, May 22, 1999.
41. Curti, *The Borrego Valley* (1955).
42. *Borrego Sun*, April, 1959.
43. The *Borrego Sun* (December, 1956) says the Anza connection is the "popularly accepted version." Al Burnand also endorses this story (as do I).
44. Personal interview, May 22, 1999.
45. *Borrego Sun*, May, 1958. The first piece of firefighting equipment stationed in the valley was an old California Division of Forestry "crash truck" which was turned over to the county for the Borrego Springs Airport in 1960. But it was not until 1962 that the Borrego Fire Protection District was formed and a volunteer fire department organized, with J. R. "Bob" Baker as its first fire chief. A one-thousand-gallon pumper was acquired, and a fire station was built in the industrial area on Stirrup Road.
46. Personal interview, March 27, 1999.
47. *Borrego Sun*, September, 1960.
48. *Borrego Sun*, April 25, 1991.
49. *Borrego Sun*, April 25, 1991.
50. Personal interview, March 27, 1999.
51. *Ramona Sentinel*, April 15, 1949.
52. The Peg Leg Smith Liars Contest began as a private affair at the home of Harry Oliver in the mid-1930s. The first public contest was held on New Year's Eve, 1948, at what is now the Peg Leg Smith Monument. After a split among the organizers in 1952, there were two Peg Leg contests each year: a new one in October at the Borrego Bowl, at the Desert Club; and the traditional New Year's Eve event at the monument. By 1955, the New Year's contest had ceased. The October contest continued until 1960. The competition was revived in 1975 by Diana Lindsay. Charlie Evans, the last winner of the old contest in 1960, also took first place in the modern contest in 1988, beating out, among others, your author, who currently holds the record for most Peg Leg victories—four. The first was a tie with Borrego motel owner Warren Boynton in 1987.

53. *Borrego Sun*, October, 1957.
54. *Borrego Sun*, November, 1960.
55. Personal interview, March 27, 1999.
56. Personal interview, March 27, 1999.
57. A personal note...it was during these years (probably in 1957 or '58) that my grandfather, Dr. Karl Brigandi, considered closing his practice in Garden Grove and reopening the medical office in Borrego Springs as a sort of semi-retirement. A private pilot, he had discovered the valley during his flights to the desert area. Unfortunately he was never able to carry out his plan, or many others. He died of cancer in 1958 at the age of 48.
58. *San Diego Evening Tribune*, April 3, 1947.
59. *Borrego Sun*, April 22, 1993.
60. Walter S. J. Swanson's history of the Copley Press, *The Thin Gold Watch* (La Jolla: The Copley Press, 1970), suggests the sale price was five hundred dollars. Bev Kuhrts remembers it as a token payment of just one dollar.
61. *Borrego Sun*, May, 1958.
62. *Borrego Sun*, December 17, 1981.
63. Personal interview, May 22, 1999.
64. *Borrego Sun*, September 13, 1990.
65. Personal interview, March 27, 1999.
66. The Downs' wedding has sometimes been called the first wedding in Borrego Springs, but it was not. On December 27, 1949, Perry Burnand married Beverly Jacobs at the Desert Lodge, with Rev. C. E. Burger of Brawley presiding (*Ramona Sentinel*, December 30, 1949).
67. *Borrego Sun*, August 2, 1990.
68. Personal interview, May 22, 1999.
69. *Borrego Sun*, November, 1953.
70. Personal interview, March 27, 1999.
71. Personal interview, October 22, 1998.

ACKNOWLEDGMENTS

When the Anza-Borrego Desert Natural History Association first approached me about writing this book, I was a little hesitant. For years I had been gathering material on the history of the Anza-Borrego Desert, and I felt quite at home with the story of the little homesteader community of Borego. But modern Borrego Springs was unknown country to me. I knew I would have a lot to learn to be able to write the second half of this book.

Researching the story of Borrego Springs has taken me down many new paths, but I was fortunate that someone else had been down those paths before me, to break trail for the rest of us. Virginia DeMarais (1915-1994) came to Borrego Springs with her husband, Bill, in 1947, and they built one of the first motels in the valley. Over the years both of them were vital, active members of the community; but more importantly, Virginia also took the time to preserve the history that was happening around them. As the years went by her files bulged with documents, newspaper clippings and photographs. For more than forty years she also wrote a regular historical feature for the *Borrego Sun* called "Do You Recall?"

I knew Virginia DeMarais only slightly, primarily through contact at the annual Borrego Founders Day reunions started by Norris Bakko in 1988, but I found her always ready, willing and able to help when asked. By leaving her files and, most valuable of all, her complete run of the *Borrego Sun* to the San Diego Historical Society, she benefited me and every Borrego researcher yet to come. It is a pity that she was not able to write the second half of this book herself, but her contributions to it are almost as rich as if she had.

It also has been my pleasure over the years to meet some of the earliest settlers in the Borrego Valley, stretching all the way back to "Doc" Beaty's only daughter, Fleta Beaty McCandless (1906-1991), who came to the valley with her parents in 1913, when the first settlers were just beginning to arrive. Her son, former Congressman Al McCandless, and his daughter, Cristina, have also been helpful to me in my research.

Most valuable of all, though, has been my friendship with Lelah Porter, who came to the valley with her husband, Milo, during the second wave of settlers in 1927. Her remarkable memory has helped me to weave together the varied strands of Borego's history, and to better understand the people of Borego and the lives they led. The Porters left the valley for Julian in 1938, and while Lelah has never regretted leaving the desert heat, she still has a soft spot for her old desert home. As this book goes to press, Lelah Porter is still living in Julian at the age of ninety-five.

There are others, too, who have contributed to my Borrego research over the years. From the early days, I must thank Lester Reed, V. F. (Bud) Clark, Margaret (Disney) Boch, Harold Ensign and Loretta Laag. Laurie Jonqueres, a descendant of the Bemis family, has also been helpful. Among the more recent Borrego pioneers, I appreciate the help and support of A. A. Burnand III, Beverly Kuhrts, Sam and Charlotte Fortiner, Catherine Strand and Leroy Shintaku.

Besides providing a safe home for the DeMarais Collection, the San Diego Historical Society Research Archives has provided a variety of other material, including oral histories from Virginia DeMarais, Norris Bakko, Sam and Charlotte Fortiner and Hank Barling. The Sherman Library and Gardens in Corona del Mar houses the papers of Horace Parker, which contain a wealth of information on the entire Anza-Borrego Desert area. Diana Lindsay has also been generous with material in her personal collection.

For contemporary published material, I have turned to the pages of the *Borrego Sun*, the *Ramona Sentinel*, the *San Diego Union*, the *Brawley News*, the Palm Springs *Desert Sun* and my own complete file of *Desert* magazine. Judy Meier, the current editor of the *Borrego Sun*, has been supportive of this project since its inception and has made scores of invaluable photographs and other material available.

This book is meant to begin where Lester Reed's classic *Old Time Cattlemen and Other Pioneers of the Anza-Borrego Area* leaves off. Hopefully someday another researcher will take on the history of Borrego Springs during the last four decades—and beyond. It's a story I will look forward to reading.

Phil Brigandi
Hemet, California
June, 2001

The Anza-Borrego Desert Natural History Association acknowledges with gratitude the enthusiasm and generosity of the A. A. Burnand Medical and Education Foundation, Ollie Cone, Judy Meier, Mr. and Mrs. Robert Reniers and Dr. and Mrs. Russell Shelden, without whose support this publication of Borrego Beginnings *would not have been possible.*

INDEX

Numbers in **bold** are photographs

ABOUT THE AUTHOR

Phil Brigandi has been researching and writing local history since 1975. He first became interested in the history of the Anza-Borrego area while working on staff at Lost Valley Scout Reservation, the Orange County Council Boy Scout summer camp in the San Ysidro Mountains, above Coyote Canyon. Since then he has written about Borrego history for the *Borrego Sun*, the *Journal of San Diego History*, and the Anza-Borrego Desert Natural History Association newsletter, *The Sand Paper*. In 1995 he completed a four hundred-page study on the history of the local livestock industry for Anza-Borrego Desert State Park.

A native of Orange, California, he has written four books on the history of his hometown, organized a local archive for the community, and was invited to join the Board of Directors of the local historical society at the tender age of eighteen. Since 1980, he has been associated with the Ramona Pageant in Hemet, and in 1990 moved to Hemet to become their Museum Curator and Pageant Historian. More recently, he also accepted the position of curator at the San Jacinto Museum. In his spare time, he continues to explore the many wonders of the Anza-Borrego Desert.